WINNING THE BATTLE
AGAINST DRUGS

WINNING THE BATTLE AGAINST DRUGS

Rehabilitation Programs

BY DANIEL MCMILLAN

FRANKLIN WATTS

NEW YORK   LONDON   TORONTO   SYDNEY
1991

Library of Congress Cataloging-in-Publication Data

McMillan, Daniel.
Winning the battle against drugs : rehabilitation programs / by
Daniel McMillan.
p. cm.
Includes bibliographical references and index.
Summary: Examines various treatments and settings for
rehabilitation of drug addicts.
ISBN 0-531-11063-X
1. Narcotic addicts—Rehabilitation—United States—Juvenile
literature. 2. Teenagers—United States—Drug use—Juvenile
literature. [1. Narcotic addicts—Rehabilitation. 2. Drug abuse.]
I. Title.
HV5809.5.M36   1991
362.29'18'0973—dc20   91-16344 CIP AC

To Mom and Dad, for all your help

CONTENTS

WINNING THE BATTLE AGAINST DRUGS

INTRODUCTION

For the past decade, the United States has been involved in a concerted campaign to eliminate (or, at least, drastically reduce) illegal drug use in this country. The effort has involved federal, state, and local authorities as well as many community organizations and private citizens. Since 1989, the antidrug movement has been bolstered by the appointment of a national drug policy coordinator (the so-called "Drug Czar"), the development of a comprehensive strategy to combat illegal drug use, and the appropriation of billions of U.S. tax dollars to fund the battle. At the same time, legislative bodies have enacted strict new laws aimed at punishing people involved in the sale or use of illegal drugs, and debates have sprung up regarding the proper role of the military in limiting the flow of foreign drugs into the United States. To most Americans, such are the sights and sounds of America's War on Drugs.

While this war has afforded politicians, military officers, and social commentators ample opportunity

11

to devise strategies for the control of illegal drugs, a less visible antidrug effort—an effort to deal with the human side of the drug problem—has quietly taken shape. This aspect of the fight against illegal drugs focuses on the rehabilitation of drug users.

Inevitably, perhaps, the people involved in rehabilitation efforts attract less attention than other participants in the drug war. Army commandos hunting down drug traffickers in Bolivia fly helicopter gunships and fire rockets into the jungle. That's the stuff of television news programs and weekly magazines. Rehabilitation counselors treating drug addicts, on the other hand, drive sedans and lead group discussions on the importance of accepting responsibility in one's life. The comparison may not be entirely fair, but it serves to illustrate a point. Drug rehabilitation is not a glitzy field, although it is something infinitely more important. It is a process that presents a possibility to a human being facing the dead-end of addiction.

Widening drug abuse and addiction is a serious challenge to American society. In cities and towns of all sizes, it can destroy families and divide neighborhoods. It can permanently impair unborn children and violently extinguish the lives of promising young people. Certainly, drug rehabilitation programs are not a magical solution to these horrible conditions. In fact, studies by the National Institute on Drug Abuse and other agencies indicate that only about half the people who complete a rehabilitation program of any kind remain free of drugs or alcohol one year later. Abstinence rates for longer periods of time are even worse. However, rehabilitation is an evolving field full of new treatment philosophies and promising methods. Rehabilitation professionals are rightfully proud of the strides they have made toward facilitating addicts' recovery, and they are hopeful that emerging techniques will bring increased success. Yet many in the drug treatment profession worry that not enough attention—or financial support—is being given to rehabilitation programs. Unless substantial new funding supplements the nation's rhetorical War on Drugs, recent rehabilitation success may be undermined.

It should be understood that this book is not offered as a singular reference on the topic of drug rehabilitation. Rather, it should be considered an overview or introduction to the subject. Further investigation of the issues presented is strongly encouraged. With that caveat, it is hoped that this book will help readers not only to understand some of the fundamental issues related to drug rehabilitation, but also to see how rehabilitation fits into the nation's overall effort to cope with illegal drugs. The topic is tremendously complex and is made even more challenging by waves of change that constantly reshape the essential problem. But, if after examining this book, readers are (1) equipped with the basic information to participate in the debate over the problems of drug dependency and rehabilitation, and (2) able to evaluate public policies regarding such topics, these words will have served their purpose.

Finally, this book could not have been completed without the assistance of the many program directors, counselors, and recovering addicts who generously shared their views on issues relating to drug rehabilitation. In addition, the reference materials available through the University of Iowa library system were invaluable in compiling factual material. The assistance of these and other people and organizations is truly appreciated.

CHAPTER ONE
AMERICA'S WAR ON DRUGS

On January 20, 1989, George Herbert Walker Bush was sworn in as the forty-first president of the United States. As usual, thousands of partisan followers flocked to Washington, D.C., to celebrate the inauguration of the new president—a reward of sorts for having endured the long electoral campaign. Indeed, in this particular year such a reward was well-deserved, as the campaign had been one of the most divisive and bitter in recent political history.

Perhaps in an effort to repair those deep divisions, Bush delivered an inaugural address that many analysts considered a blueprint for reconciliation and compromise. Effective policy making depended, he said, on cooperation between rival political parties and understanding among the many branches of government. His administration would provide an environment for such cooperation, he pledged. In the international arena, too, the new chief executive held out hope for continued improvement in relations with the Soviet Union, a nation his predecessor, Ronald Reagan, had once termed "The Evil Empire." As he took the oath of office, Bush declared: "A new breeze is blowing and the old bipartisanship must be made new again. . . . I put out my hand." To the tens of thousands of spectators gathered at the west front of the Capitol and the millions of others watching on television, it seemed George Bush might actually deliver on his vision of a "kinder, gentler nation" after all.

The tone of reconciliation, flexibility, and gentleness quickly vanished, however, as the new president turned to the topic of drug abuse. The nation's security was threatened, Bush said, by the use of illegal drugs and its devastating effect on the whole of society. Speaking deliberately and with the type of purposefulness leaders usually reserve for only the gravest of crises, Bush stared intently into the television cameras and pronounced: "Take my word. This scourge will stop." There could be no doubt that the drug issue was on the presidential agenda.

Eight months later, further evidence of the growing political importance of drugs came when Bush appeared on television for the first prime-time, nationwide address of his presidency. The sole topic: drug abuse.

"This is the first time since taking the oath of office that I felt an issue was so important, so threatening, that it warranted talking directly with you, the American people," Bush began. "All of us agree that the gravest domestic threat facing our nation today is drugs."

In this long-awaited speech, Bush went on to outline a $7.9 billion antidrug strategy that included plans for tougher punishment of illegal drug users, increased drug testing, expanded education and prevention campaigns, and economic aid to the struggling South American nations responsible for most of the illegal drug production.

"This plan is as comprehensive as the problem,"

the president said. "Our weapons in this strategy are: the law and criminal justice system; our foreign policy; our treatment systems; and our schools and drug prevention programs." Overall, about 70 percent of the resources of the Bush plan were aimed at containing the drug supply and enforcing laws against illegal drugs. The remaining 30 percent was allocated for treatment and prevention programs. The plan had both critics and proponents. Many, particularly those in the drug treatment community, felt more resources should have been devoted to rehabilitation services.

Convincing evidence that the war on drugs was more than a catchy phrase came in the early morning hours of December 20, 1989. In the largest American military action since its involvement in Vietnam, U.S. armed forces invaded the Central American nation of Panama and toppled the government of General Manuel Antonio Noriega, who had been indicted in the United States on drug trafficking charges. Noriega surrendered to American officials and was flown to Miami to face trial in U.S. Federal Court. Although the invasion of Panama involved other issues in addition to drugs, Noriega's connections to drug cartels intensified the American desire to remove him from power. The massive show of force in Panama underscored the seriousness of the drug war.

These events—a comprehensive drug strategy, a multibillion dollar budget to combat drug abuse, tough new laws to punish illegal drug users, and military action against foreign governments allegedly involved in drug trafficking—are among the more recent and visible developments in the American war on drugs. The roots of this antidrug movement run deep, however, drawing strength from a wide variety of sources.

The present environment has emerged gradually as attitudes about drug use have evolved and

CHART 1

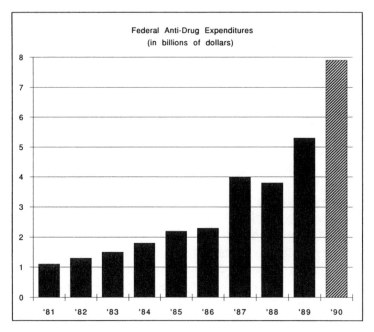

Federal Anti-Drug Expenditures
(in billions of dollars)

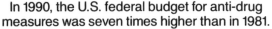

In 1990, the U.S. federal budget for anti-drug
measures was seven times higher than in 1981.

changed. In the past, it has sometimes been tolerated
and sometimes condemned. But today, an overwhelming majority of Americans consider drug
abuse a unique and unqualified danger to the nation.
In September 1989, a New York Times/CBS News
public opinion poll found that 64 percent of Americans felt drugs were the most important problem
facing the country. Not only was this the highest
percentage registered for any single issue since the
two news organizations began polling in 1976, but
it was also one of the highest percentages ever
recorded in any national survey. By comparison, the
economy—second on the list of most pressing na-

18

tional problems—was cited by only 5 percent of respondents. Drugs were far and away the leading problem. A host of other surveys in 1989 and 1990, including one of civic officials conducted by the National League of Cities, also found drug abuse to be the nation's number one problem.

Admittedly, public opinion polls are but momentary glimpses of ever-changing attitudes. (In a similar New York Times/CBS News poll in July 1989, only 22 percent of Americans called drugs the most serious problem facing the nation.) However, few will dispute that the drug issue has captured the nation's attention and will likely remain a top political priority for the foreseeable future.

Just what is "the drug problem" and how did it become an issue of the highest importance, elevated above other national concerns like economic vitality, military strength, educational excellence, and environmental safety? Furthermore, how did the drug issue capture such attention, particularly at a time when overall drug use appears to be on the decline in the United States?[1] These questions are complex and require some further analysis.

GETTING A HANDLE ON THE DRUG PROBLEM

To fully understand the present antidrug climate in the United States, it is helpful to have some mental picture of what constitutes the drug problem. Unfortunately, constructing such a mental image is not easy because the scope of the American drug problem is rather difficult to define. For one thing, the problem is not caused by a single drug that can be isolated and stamped out.

Although substances like crack cocaine dominate the newspaper headlines, there are literally hundreds of illegal *psychoactive* drugs available on the street today. Unlike ordinary prescription medications, which are taken to fight diseases or relieve symptoms, psychoactive drugs are used to temporarily alter the body's central nervous system. Different drugs have different effects. *Uppers*, such as cocaine and amphetamines, stimulate the central nervous system and make the user feel increased levels of energy. Conversely, *downers*, from opium to alcohol, act as depressants that tend to slow down or desensitize the central nervous system. (Depressants have legitimate uses as painkillers in hospitals and dental offices.) Another variety of drugs known as *hallucinogens* or *psychedelics* are also part of the problem. These drugs include marijuana, LSD, and a variety of other naturally occurring substances. The primary effect of these drugs is to temporarily alter consciousness and change the way the user interprets his or her surroundings. A fourth category of drugs is that known as *dissociative anesthetics*, such as PCP (angel dust). These drugs have longer-lasting, more intense effects than the ones described above. Under the influence of these drugs, the user typically experiences complete separation from reality for extended periods of time.

In addition to the vast array of drugs already on the street, the rapid development of new illegal substances only makes the scope of the drug problem more difficult to grasp. In the early 1980s, crack cocaine, for example, was virtually unheard of. Today it is largely responsible for the alarming rise in the rate of cocaine addiction in the United States. Methamphetamines (also known as "crank" or "crystal") are another example. These extremely potent drugs can be manufactured at home with a few readily available chemicals, and their use is spreading quickly.

Many people argue that America's drug problem also includes such legal drugs as alcohol and nicotine (the active substance found in tobacco products). Use of these accepted drugs is much more widespread than any illegal substance and the cost to society for such habits is very high. While controversial, there is some merit in the view that alcohol and tobacco are legitimate targets in a campaign against drugs. Consider the fact that drunk drivers are responsible for about 50 percent of all motor vehicle fatalities nationwide. Or consider that tobacco use prematurely claims the lives of 400,000 Americans every year. Or that the United States Surgeon General says cigarette smoking is the number one cause of death and disease in the world's developed nations. Naturally, everyone—not just alcohol and tobacco users—pays the price for the abuse of these legal drugs. The U.S. Department of Health and Human Services Office of Smoking and Health estimates that in 1985 America's smoking habit cost every man, woman, and child in this country $205. That's what it cost to pay for smokers' added health costs and lower productivity on the job.

Most of the information in this book will pertain to the abuse of illegal drugs, such as cocaine, heroin, and marijuana. However, in profiling drug rehabilitation programs, it is necessary to confront other addictive drugs, including alcohol, which according to the National Institute on Drug Abuse, is the most widely abused substance in the United States.

Finally, when constructing a mental picture of the drug problem one must also take into account the various degrees of drug abuse that occur throughout society. The different degrees are like separate elements and one must decide which elements to include in the picture: Is everyone who uses drugs—even the so-called casual drug user who smokes an occasional marijuana joint in the privacy of his or her own home—considered part of the problem? Or is the drug problem made up only of those individ-

CHART 2

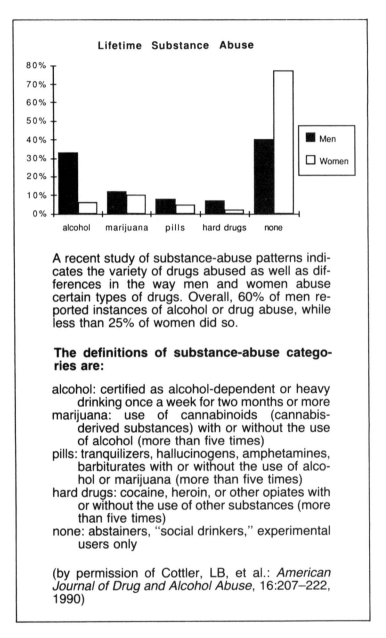

Lifetime Substance Abuse

Men

Women

alcohol   marijuana   pills   hard drugs   none

A recent study of substance-abuse patterns indicates the variety of drugs abused as well as differences in the way men and women abuse certain types of drugs. Overall, 60% of men reported instances of alcohol or drug abuse, while less than 25% of women did so.

The definitions of substance-abuse categories are:

alcohol: certified as alcohol-dependent or heavy drinking once a week for two months or more

marijuana: use of cannabinoids (cannabis-derived substances) with or without the use of alcohol (more than five times)

pills: tranquilizers, hallucinogens, amphetamines, barbiturates with or without the use of alcohol or marijuana (more than five times)

hard drugs: cocaine, heroin, or other opiates with or without the use of other substances (more than five times)

none: abstainers, "social drinkers," experimental users only

(by permission of Cottler, LB, et al.: *American Journal of Drug and Alcohol Abuse*, 16:207–222, 1990)

uals who are deeply involved in illegal drugs—
smugglers, dealers, addicts, and so on? Should a dis-
tinction be made between these groups of people
and, if so, where should the line be drawn? Like the
many kinds of illegal drugs on the street, the constant development of new drugs, and the debate over
legal drugs like alcohol and tobacco products, the
issue of casual use makes defining the drug problem
even more tricky.

MOTIVATING THE WAR ON DRUGS

If defining the drug problem is complex, explaining
the reasons behind the rise in public apprehension
over drug use is even more complicated. Some of the
aspects of drug use that prompt concern are discussed below.

The Crime Connection

One major motivator of public concern is the
close association between drugs, crime, and violence. In large cities, and increasingly in smaller
communities, the level of drug-related crime is sky-
rocketing, according to law enforcement authorities
nationwide. In Detroit, for example, the district at-
torney's office estimates that 70 percent of all crimes
in the area are drug related. In Washington, D.C.,
now the nation's murder capital as well as its political capital, homicide hit an all-time high in 1989
with 438 murders; police estimate that more than 50
percent were connected to disputes involving drugs.
Other cities across the nation, from Philadelphia to
Kansas City and Dallas, also set new homicide
records in 1990, and drugs were blamed for much of
the increase. Preliminary figures put the total number of homicide victims at 23,220 for 1990—the highest total in U.S. history.

Sadly, the rising death tolls often involved innocent bystanders, people who were neither drug dealers nor drug users, but just happened to be in the wrong place at the wrong time. While statistics for such "stray-bullet" deaths are not kept by local police departments or the Federal Bureau of Investigation, the Washington, D.C.-based Crime Control Institute (CCI) published a report in 1989 showing a dramatic rise in these types of killings. In New York, thirty bystanders lost their lives in 1989 and many more were wounded. In Los Angeles, the CCI found, no bystander deaths were noted from 1983 to 1985, but in 1988 twenty-one such slayings occurred. Often the victims were children who unknowingly wandered into the line of danger. Others were pedestrians gunned down on the sidewalk, caught in the crossfire. Sometimes victims didn't even leave their homes; at least one man in New York was killed by a ricocheting bullet while asleep in his bed. The people of New York City, who have grown relatively accustomed to street violence, were shocked in the summer of 1990 by a particularly terrifying string of shootings: between July 22 and September 23 no less than twenty-two children were shot in random gun attacks. Law enforcement officials and other community leaders attribute most of the increase in stray-bullet deaths to the easy availability of high-powered weapons and drug-dealing activity.

"The drug gangs have set the tone that life is very cheap," said Thomas Reppetto, head of New York City's Citizens Crime Commission, in an interview with the *New York Times*. This explanation is supported by the CCI report, which indicated that the fastest growing category of bystander deaths is the "drive-by" shooting, the method drug gangs typically use to mark out their turf by firing into crowds from a passing vehicle.

Another factor contributing to the public's fear

is the fact that drug warriors perpetrate their violent acts with some of the most sophisticated weapons on the market. Police raids of drug hideouts regularly turn up AK-47 assault rifles, 9 mm automatic pistols, and Uzi submachine guns. And in the high-stakes trafficking business, drug rings have shown a willingness to use deadly force against anyone who tries to interrupt their lucrative trade. The 1985 torture and slaying of U.S. Drug Enforcement Agent Ricardo Camareno in Guadalajara, Mexico, made the brutal point that even federal law enforcement officials were fair game. Coupled with the Camareno murder and reports that the number of police officers killed in drug-related incidents has reached record levels,[2] the drug runners' arsenals give rise to the question: Will law enforcement officers be able to keep the upper hand?

The media—television, newspapers, magazines, and radio—amplify the "fear factor" by bringing the menace of drug violence into the life of anyone who can watch, read, or listen. Thanks to an all-out media blitz, it's no longer necessary to live in an inner city housing project to understand the tragedy of the drug epidemic. Television programs chronicle the sad, and frequently very short, lives of kids who grow up running drugs for older pushers, or the even sadder, shorter lives of abnormal babies born to cocaine-using mothers. Such television images, not to mention the constant stream of articles in newspapers and magazines, have made a powerful impact on the American people and, consequently, have helped push the drug issue to the top of the priority list.

A Deadly Epidemic

In contrast to the obvious threat posed by drug gangs and crack houses, a more insidious drug-related menace began to stir the nation in the early 1980s with the first reports of a deadly, incurable disease: Acquired Immune Deficiency Syndrome—AIDS. Researchers discovered that the disease was caused by a virus (the human immunodeficiency virus or HIV) carried in bodily fluids and that the virus destroyed the human immune system. The first symptoms of AIDS can include skin rashes, fever, and weight loss, but as the disease progresses the patient usually develops cancer and other serious illnesses that lead to death. Nearly a decade after its recognition in the United States, there is still no vaccine to prevent its spread and no effective treatment to save those already infected.

In the early years of the AIDS epidemic, many people considered it a "homosexual" disease. Soon, however, it was learned that the disease could afflict anyone engaged in certain "high-risk" behaviors. High-risk groups typically include homosexuals, bisexuals, heterosexuals with multiple sex partners, hemophiliacs, and intravenous (IV)-drug users. Health care workers treating AIDS patients are also at risk of infection through exposure to bodily fluids like blood. IV-drug users, such as those who inject heroin, are among its most likely victims because in the common practice of sharing needles and syringes AIDS-tainted blood is passed from one user to the next.

Re-use of contaminated needles and syringes is one of the leading means of transmitting the AIDS virus. Today, it is estimated that IV-drug users account for about one of every five AIDS patients. Furthermore, the number of IV-drug users diagnosed with the AIDS virus is growing faster than other high-risk groups, according to the U.S. Centers for Disease Control. From 1981 to 1987, IV-drug users comprised approximately 18 percent of the annually reported AIDS cases, but in 1989 their share jumped to nearly 24 percent. And many experts believe AIDS will continue to increase among IV-drug users. As researcher

Dr. Fred Rosner of the State University of New York observes: "The main projected increase in AIDS patients over the next few years is precisely in this group of people [IV-drug users]. Homosexuals, but not drug abusers, are changing their life-style to reduce the risk of AIDS."[3]

By the end of 1990, the U.S. Centers for Disease Control had received 154,791 reports of AIDS cases. The U.S. Public Health Service projects that by 1992 the total number of documented AIDS cases in the United States will exceed 200,000. Meanwhile, the World Health Organization estimates that 5 to 10 million persons throughout the world have been infected with the AIDS virus and that within five years about 1 million new AIDS cases will be diagnosed. These numbers, staggering by themselves, are even more sobering when it is considered that HIV can be present in a person for five to ten years before the onset of AIDS symptoms. That means many more people infected with the virus, but not yet suffering its effects, are likely to be diagnosed with the disease in coming years.

The cost of treating AIDS patients is also a major concern. "Aggressively treated" AIDS patients—those who receive zidovudine or costly experimental medications as well as multiple X rays, blood tests, and professional consultations—frequently run up bills of several hundred thousand dollars in the course of their treatment. Such bills can bankrupt those burdened with payment: families, hospitals, even insurance companies. According to conservative estimates, the AIDS epidemic is projected to have cost the United States more than $6 billion in 1990.

Not only are IV-drug users with AIDS growing in number, but the cost of treating these AIDS patients is usually higher. "Intravenous drug users with AIDS are more expensive to care for because they often lack social, financial, and material support," states SUNY's Dr. Rosner.

According to Dr. Mary E. Chamberland of the Centers for Disease Control, drug treatment facilities have a major role in combating the AIDS epidemic. "The primary strategy for reducing HIV infection associated with IV-drug use must be providing adequate and effective drug treatment programs," she notes.[4]

Significantly, the AIDS epidemic has put everyone at risk, not only IV-drug users or homosexuals or those directly involved in the treatment of infected individuals. Although these high-risk groups remain the most likely to contract the disease, other activities, such as receiving a blood transfusion, can have life-threatening consequences. Throughout the United States, the Red Cross and individual hospitals have instituted extensive screening and testing programs to ensure the safety of the blood supply, but infections cannot always be avoided, and new strains of the virus can escape detection. Technical malfunctions and human error can conspire to release tainted blood into the supply system. Although the blood supply is believed to be generally safe, AIDS-contamination remains a major concern at every hospital, clinic, and doctor's office.

A Society At Risk

Another force behind the public outcry against illegal drugs is the "fear factor" on a much larger scale. Whereas the type of fear described above relates primarily to personal well-being—fear of being shot, assaulted, infected, and so on, because of drugs—this type of fear relates to social well-being. This is the fear that in addition to menacing individuals, drug abuse will eventually corrupt entire societies and thereby threaten to spread destruction far beyond those directly involved with drugs.

This anxiety is fueled by indictments against elected leaders like Washington, D.C., Mayor Marion Barry for drug-related activities; by the Colombian drug cartels' assassination of that country's judges, legislators, and top government officials; and by the growing list of U.S. law enforcement agents accused of involvement in illegal drug deals. The 1988 arrest and conviction of Matthew Barnwell, a New York City public school principal, on charges of buying crack cocaine also brought the corruption issue home to many people. With the massive profits of the drug trade, it is feared that even the highest government officials and most trusted public servants can be corrupted.

The use of drugs in the workplace also sparks controversy. The Partnership for a Drug-Free America estimates that in 1987 alone, U.S. businesses lost more than $60 billion through employee drug abuse. That is money lost through absenteeism, reduced productivity while on the job, health problems resulting from drug abuse, and the like. In addition to these enormous financial losses, public safety has in some instances been put at risk by drug-impaired employees. One of the most highly publicized cases involved the 1987 wreck of an Amtrak passenger train near Baltimore, Maryland, in which sixteen people died when their train slammed into a misguided freight locomotive. A government investigation of the accident later revealed that the engineer of the freight train, who admitted to using marijuana and other drugs, had ignored a stop signal and had steered his locomotive onto the wrong track. More recently, attention has been drawn to this same issue by the trial of three Northwest Airlines pilots charged with flying passenger jets while under the influence of alcohol. (According to records kept by the Federal Aviation Administration, the public may have every reason to be unnerved by alcohol abuse among airline pilots. The FAA says that about 1,200 active pilots have been treated for alcoholism since 1975.) Based on such experiences, people begin to question whether other workers—perhaps even those in the most sensitive jobs, such as air traffic controllers or police officers—might be using drugs on the job, too. What about technicians at nuclear power plants or military installations? Doctors, nurses, school-bus drivers? The potential consequences of a drug-impaired workforce are frightening.

The list of fears and concerns prompted by the spread of illegal drugs is very long indeed. Those mentioned in this chapter are just some of the many issues that have convinced so many people in the United States that there is a serious drug problem in this country. If not directly affected by stray-bullet killings or infected blood supplies or drugs in the workplace, most people are frightened by some other aspect of spreading drug use. Maybe the drug trade has eroded the sense of security and trust that once held their neighborhood together. Maybe their local schools have become havens for drug dealing instead of learning. Or maybe it's the fact that they no longer feel safe flying in airplanes or even riding the subway to work because of the drug situation. The important point is that these varied threats have, over time, combined to make a great many people feel very unsafe.

Because the threat has affected them in so many different ways, the American people have come to believe some type of response is necessary. And political leaders are scrambling to formulate that response in laws and public policies. Briefly, this is how our nation has developed its present attitude about illegal drug use and this is why leaders from President Bush on down to city mayors have declared the so-called "War on Drugs."

In fighting this war, the nation is mobilizing many different forces. In addition to hiring more police officers, enacting stricter laws, and building more prisons, one of the primary weapons being used in the battle against illegal drug use is treatment for addiction. The federal, state, and local governments are financing some rehabilitation programs, but private groups are also involved. Many businesses have established Employee Assistance Programs to help workers deal with drugs (and other personal problems). Churches have also set up programs to involve their members in drug rehabilitation and/or prevention plans, and so have many private hospitals and groups like the YMCA/YWCA and Narcotics Anonymous. By helping people with drug addictions to overcome their dependency, many people believe that the multiple threats associated with the drug problem can be reduced or eliminated. Crime rates can be lowered, schools can concentrate on educating students, the spread of AIDS can be slowed, businesses can operate more efficiently: in general, people can lead safer, more productive lives.

In this book, the primary philosophies of drug rehabilitation will be examined and the role of treatment in confronting the nation's drug problem will be explained.

CHAPTER TWO
TREATMENT OPTIONS FOR DRUG DEPENDENCY

Each of us walks a path in life. For most of us that path has many branches. Each branch represents a choice—perhaps a turning point, or a joining of one path with another, one person with another.

The chemically dependent person follows a different path. The force of addiction to alcohol or other drugs gradually blinds that person to the choices in life. Their path narrows. It is an empty path.

Treatment for chemical dependency stops the addicted person in their hopeless routine. Slowly, with the help of others, that person begins to see a new direction. It is the path of sobriety.

The first steps on that path can be difficult. But with practice, it becomes easier to travel. It widens. New branches appear. In time, the path is filled with the richness of recovery.

—Hazelden Rehabilitation Services

In recent years, the phrase "drug rehabilitation" has become so widely used that it may be surprising to learn that the concept of successfully treating individuals for addiction is a relatively new idea. Forty years ago drug addiction was thought to be untreatable and the notion of rehabilitating a substance abuser was as unheard of as withdrawing money from an automatic teller machine in a shopping mall.

Certainly, drug abuse treatment is still a controversial topic, but arguments usually pertain to which methods are most effective and how to make it more accessible to those who need it. The basic concept that therapy can enable individuals with substance abuse or dependency problems to lead improved or drug-free lives is not widely disputed. Acceptance of treatment as an option for addicts, however, only came about after centuries of experimentation with various substances and only after addiction itself was more fully understood by medical professionals.

DRUG USE AND ATTEMPTED CURES

The history of man's experimentation with "drugs" is long and colorful. The use of coca, from which cocaine is derived, can be traced back to at least 2500 B.C. when the natives of South America chewed on leaves from the coca plant. Chewing the leaves, they discovered, resulted in numerous "desirable" effects, including increased strength and endurance. Native peoples of North America also made use of various hallucinogenic substances in religious rituals. Morphine, heroin, and other *opiates* (drugs derived from opium) were popular in the United States throughout the nineteenth century. Widely used in both prescription medicines and patent medicines that claimed to cure all ills, opiates crept into the everyday lives of many ordinary citizens; the "relaxing, euphoric" qualities of these narcotics made them ideal painkillers. In the late 1800s and early 1900s, cocaine became popular and, in addition to its use in medications for ailments such as arthritis and hay fever, it was an ingredient in many consumer products. (The name Coca-Cola® comes from the fact that this popular beverage contained cocaine when it first came onto the market in 1886. Another cocaine-laced soft drink of the late nineteenth century carried the name Dope Cola!) In short, the use of mind- or mood-altering substances far pre-dates the stereotypical hippie drug addict of the 1960s.

In response to Americans' changing drug habits, approaches to treating drug addiction have also developed. Initially, opium-derived drugs like morphine and heroin were targeted and treatment for these substances was usually carried out in hospitals. Often, many of these early attempts at treatment failed due to a basic misunderstanding of the substances involved. For instance, early twentieth-century physicians believed cocaine could actually cure opium addiction and alcoholism; in the course of such "treatment," cocaine was substituted for these other drugs because it was not considered addictive. Patients "cured" in this way simply exchanged one addiction for another.

With advancing scientific knowledge and changing attitudes in the past forty years, new philosophies about addiction and options for treating it have developed. The notion that addiction is a type of moral failing still has some adherents today, but more and more people have come to regard addiction as a disease, a chronic problem that can be treated and controlled, if not cured. Modern researchers have also tried to shed light on addiction by investigating concepts such as addictive personalities and internal chemical imbalances—situations that may predispose some individuals to addiction. As more has been learned about addiction, possibilities for treatment have grown. One of the most widely used rehabilitation approaches to emerge is the Twelve Steps program of Alcoholics Anonymous. The Twelve Steps, which have been adapted by other groups like Narcotics Anonymous[1] and Cocaine Anonymous, are a self-help guide for those recovering from addiction. Many independent drug rehabilitation programs have also incorporated the Twelve Steps concepts into their treatment plans. Briefly, these programs are designed to overcome addiction through reliance on "a higher power" and on the support of similarly addicted individuals. (A more thorough discussion of the Twelve Steps and Narcotics Anonymous is found in Chapter 7.)

THE PRESENT TREATMENT NETWORK

Based on the idea that treatment can, in fact, reduce or eliminate drug abuse, a network of rehabilitation programs has emerged in the United States. This network consists of approximately 650,000 rehabilitation programs nationwide, which deal with everything from cocaine and heroin addiction to alcoholism and barbiturate abuse. Within some boundaries, the majority of drug rehabilitation programs available today fall into one of the following categories: inpatient/residential rehabilitation communities (also known as therapeutic communities), outpatient drug-free programs, and methadone maintenance clinics.

In inpatient communities, individuals undergoing treatment live in a group setting and receive nearly round-the-clock attention to their substance abuse problems. These programs offer a comprehensive treatment approach with the ultimate goal of totally overhauling the drug abuser's life-style. They stress drug-free living, the development of social and work-related skills, and the acceptance of personal responsibility. These programs are typically long-term, ranging from several weeks to several months or more in duration, and tend to be the most expensive form of drug rehabilitation.

The environment in inpatient communities is usually very highly structured. Clients must participate in assigned activities each day and make steady progress through the various phases of the treatment program. Each phase requires the individual to accept additional responsibilities, such as leading discussions, and may also allow for extra privileges, such as free time away from the residential facility.

Group counseling is also emphasized in this treatment setting and it is not unusual for these discussions to develop into heated arguments. In fact, confrontation is an important part of the treatment philosophy in many residential programs. By forcing clients (many of whom are referred there by the criminal justice system) to face up to their desperate personal situations, rather than escaping through the use of drugs, these treatment centers aim to help clients build healthier life-styles that are based on honesty, openness, and responsibility. The participation of peer-counselors, many of whom are graduates of rehabilitation programs, is also common in inpatient communities. Such individuals can act as excellent role models, and they often have a better understanding of the reasons behind a drug abuser's problems.

Another distinguishing feature of inpatient treatment programs is their usually strong commitment to clients' reentry into society following completion of the rehabilitation program. This process, known as "resocialization," helps the client integrate back into the culture and resume a productive life-style. The extent to which these programs attempt to "resocialize" addicts varies. Some strive for clients' complete, unsupervised re-entry into mainstream society. Others limit their emphasis to rebuilding personal relationships and maintaining drug abstinence. Naturally, the degree of resocialization sought is one factor determining the length of time the client remains in treatment.

As a group, outpatient programs are the most popular and least expensive form of drug treatment in the United States today. These programs vary widely in terms of services offered and in their approach to rehabilitation. In general, however, they tend to be community-based organizations that emphasize counseling via social workers and psychiatrists. Many outpatient treatment programs are affiliated with a local hospital or mental health center and some offer a variety of companion services, including legal advice, job training, and basic educational opportunities.

In this type of rehabilitation, clients visit a treatment center on a scheduled basis and take part in programs to reduce their dependence on drugs while trying to lead basically normal lives outside of treatment. Usually, individuals continue to live at home and hold a job or attend school. The treatment program may include daily classes and individualized counseling for one or two weeks and then another two to four weeks of meeting less frequently (three to five times per week perhaps).

Unlike most inpatient treatment centers, resocialization is not always the long-term goal of outpatient programs. Although data is sparse, most are believed to be geared toward helping addicts develop basic coping skills and drug-free life-styles rather than complete resocialization.

Clients in outpatient treatment programs are usually people addicted to cocaine or alcohol rather than opium-derived drugs.

*   *   *

Methadone maintenance clinics are treatment programs that center around the use of *methadone hydrochloride*, a synthetic drug, as a substitute for heroin. Researchers have found that the use of methadone on a daily basis satisfies the heroin addict's intense craving for an opiate drug without causing the disabling side effects associated with heroin. Its supporters say this characteristic of methadone allows addicts to reestablish relatively normal, productive lives. In addition, methadone effectively blocks the "high" associated with heroin, so addicts receiving this synthetic drug have less incentive to return to heroin use. Given the fact that heroin addiction is among the most difficult to overcome, as well as the high risk of AIDS transmission associated with IV-drug abuse, methadone treatment has been justified by some in the treatment community as a "necessary evil."

Since its introduction in the 1960s, methadone has been very controversial. Critics claim that methadone patients are simply addicts of another drug. This negative view of methadone treatment may stem from the fact that many clinics do not always strive for clients' eventual abstinence. Long-term methadone use is an acceptable outcome of treatment for some addicts, according to methadone specialists. Some methadone patients, however, do eventually achieve abstinence.

Despite criticism, methadone use has continued and, according to its advocates, is more successful than any other form of treatment for heroin addicts. In contrast to inpatient communities, methadone clinics are almost always run on an outpatient basis.

Within each of the three major treatment options—inpatient/residential communities, outpatient programs, and methadone maintenance clinics—there are a variety of persistent controversies. In order to fully understand these controversies, it should be realized that drug rehabilitation is a developing, evolving field, not an established set of rules that are easily applied to each and every situation. For one thing, the problem that drug rehabilitation programs are responding to—addiction—involves issues that are very difficult to define: personality, motivation, desire, frustration, and so on. The rehabilitation movement is also complicated by the regular appearance of new drugs, which necessitate the development of new treatment philosophies. The result is that some approaches used even a few years ago are no longer considered valid, and today's techniques may be obsolete next year. Finally, the current drug problems in the United States are different from previous situations. The population in need of treatment is unique both in size and in demographic makeup. Society is just beginning to learn how to deal with these challenges. In this subjective, ever-changing environment, controversies are inevitable.

EFFECTIVENESS

A major controversy relating to drug rehabilitation today is the issue of effectiveness: what is the best method of treatment for substance abusers? This issue is extremely complex because it involves so many factors. For instance, to determine the effectiveness of a given drug rehabilitation program, one must attempt to evaluate:

- the types of clients the program serves
- the style of treatment provided
- the background and competency of those delivering treatment

- changes resulting from treatment versus changes stemming from other causes
- the length of time clients remain drug-free after completing the treatment program

Tremendous diversity exists within each one of these points, not to mention the many others too numerous to list here. To examine just one, consider the types of clients the program serves. Obviously, the variation here is virtually limitless. Some clients are dependent on cocaine, others heroin, alcohol, amphetamines, hallucinogens, marijuana, tranquilizers, or a combination of these and other drugs. The severity of addiction also varies. Clients may range in age from teens or younger to elderly adults. They can be married or single, high school dropouts or college professors. Perhaps they've been referred through the criminal justice system or maybe they've come of their own free will. Each one of these variables has implications for the effectiveness of a given rehabilitation program.

As noted earlier, rehabilitation centers are usually set up as either inpatient or outpatient programs. There are several facets to the debate over inpatient versus outpatient treatment, one of which is the respective success rates of the two styles of rehabilitation. Advocates of outpatient treatment argue that keeping individuals in their natural environment—in the company of their family and friends, on their job, etc.—forces recovering addicts to face "real world" situations. According to this line of reasoning, inpatient programs shield addicts too much from normal pressures and only set them up for failure when they are finally released from treatment. In contrast, proponents of inpatient treatment contend that separation of the addict from his or her environment is crucial to successful rehabilitation. Only by being physically removed from the situations that promote drug abuse and being taught to cope with difficulties in a responsible way can addicts hope to return to normal living.

At the present time, information on the success rates of inpatient and outpatient rehabilitation is extremely difficult to gather since most treatment centers either do not keep such statistics or are unwilling to share them with people outside of the program.

COST

Another part of the continuing debate over treatment programs relates to the benefits derived from drug rehabilitation in relation to the expenditures required to achieve those benefits. The cost issue can be broken down into two basic parts: (1) Is drug rehabilitation, in general, cost effective? (2) If it is, which form of treatment is most efficient?

To answer the first part, it is necessary to weigh the cost of drug rehabilitation against the cost of continued drug addiction. While it is impossible to determine precise dollar amounts for these costs, it is possible to make some estimates. The United States spends about $3 billion per year on drug abuse treatment. This figure includes the amount that federal, state, and local governments spend for rehabilitation programs, as well as the amount paid out by private insurance companies and individuals. Against this $3 billion must be weighed the multiple costs to society that result from continued drug addiction. Some of the major expenses associated with drug use are:

• medical bills for addicts, children born to drug-using mothers, and IV-drug users who contract AIDS
• the cost of drug-related crimes, including property losses and legal expenses

- reduced productivity among the drug-impaired workers

Numerous studies have attempted to calculate these expenses. In the final analysis, many experts predict substantial economic benefits could be obtained from increased use of drug rehabilitation.

The second part of the cost issue focuses on the form of treatment that is most efficient. Considering the variety of illegal drugs on the street, it is unrealistic to say any one treatment approach is best in all cases. Different addictions require different methods of treatment. However, as with the effectiveness debate, the issue of cost often boils down to a decision between inpatient and outpatient treatment. Inpatient treatment is by its very nature much more expensive than outpatient treatment. Whether it is in a hospital, group home, or other residential rehabilitation facility, the inpatient client lives away from home and must be fed, housed, and closely monitored by a professional staff. A typical inpatient treatment program lasting thirty days can cost from $5,000 to $15,000. Outpatient services are much less costly, rarely exceeding $3,000. Since outpatient clients continue to live at home and hold jobs or attend school, they generally pay their own living expenses. The unique advantages and disadvantages of the different treatment approaches will be discussed in subsequent chapters.

ACCESSIBILITY

One of the biggest concerns relating to drug rehabilitation is accessibility—drug treatment programs must be made available to those who need them. Throughout the United States today, the number of people in need of drug rehabilitation is estimated to be about 5.5 million, which is far greater than the number of openings in treatment centers. Waiting lists as long as one to two years are not uncommon, especially in urban areas. The result is that most people with drug problems go untreated. In fact, according to the Alcohol, Drug Abuse and Mental Health Administration, only about one of every seven individuals with a serious drug problem ever receives treatment. In many inner cities, where crack cocaine and heroin addiction is highest, drug treatment programs are virtually nonexistent.

Particularly desperate are the many addicted women, who generally have even fewer options than their male counterparts. While women comprise almost 60 percent of the estimated 9.5 million drug users in the United States, many programs today serve only men. This inequity stems from the fact that men have traditionally been identified with drug and alcohol abuse while women have not. As the statistics illustrate, however, times have changed.

Access to drug treatment is scarce for women in general, but it is even more so for pregnant women and women with children. Nationwide, there are only a handful of treatment programs geared toward this population. In some areas, this dilemma is so severe that civil rights organizations have filed lawsuits to force programs to open their doors to such women. Meanwhile, many observers warn that this aspect of the drug problem may be the most threatening because when pregnant women or those with children are denied drug treatment, the damage of drug dependency is passed on to the next generation.

Unborn babies are especially vulnerable because substances that enter the mother's body are passed directly to the fetus—usually in higher concentrations. Recent medical research indicates that if a woman uses cocaine *even once* during pregnancy, her baby may suffer deformity, brain damage, and possibly even stroke. Some experts estimate that between 1988 and 1991, one million drug-exposed babies will be born in the United States. The cost of medical care during their infancy could be as much as $100,000 per child.

Understanding the many sides of the drug abuse problem helps to place drug rehabilitation efforts into their proper perspective. As described earlier, relevant parts of the story include the long history of substance use and abuse as well as the unique social problems of today. Beyond these points, it should be recognized that each of the major treatment styles —inpatient/residential communities, outpatient programs, and methadone clinics—has certain advantages and disadvantages.

With this background, it is possible to isolate some fundamental goals that all rehabilitation programs try to achieve:

• Keep the client in treatment. The dropout rate is usually highest in the early stages of rehabilitation.
• Teach (or strengthen existing) personal qualities such as honesty, responsibility, and self-esteem.
• Help the client understand how his or her dependency on drugs developed.
• Provide clients with the survival skills necessary to establish and maintain a life-style that does not revolve around drug use. Such skills may include basic education (reading, writing, math) and job training.
• Provide follow-up, aftercare, or other ongoing services to reduce the likelihood of relapse.

Although rehabilitation holds great promise, the problem of drug dependency is tremendously complex and drug treatment is far from a perfect science. The less-than-glowing success rate for treatment (as noted, about 50 percent) is due in large part to the fact that therapy for addiction is still a developing technique, much of which depends on subjective assessments of personality and motivation as well as individual desire to change. Each person entering into treatment is unique and the factors that will enable that person to overcome addiction are only partially understood. There is not—nor can there be—a formula for the successful rehabilitation of a drug addict.

However, while the precise role of rehabilitation in relation to other antidrug efforts is still being established, its importance cannot be disputed. In a span of less than forty years, drug rehabilitation has progressed to a point at which it now offers hope to thousands of addicts. It is reasonable to expect that, in time, additional rehabilitation techniques will be developed or refined that will make drug treatment an even more important tool in reducing drug use.

CHAPTER THREE
DRUG REHABILITATION IN RESIDENTIAL AND OUTPATIENT SETTINGS

Two hundred eighty-eight acres of woods and rolling hills in east central Minnesota may not seem a likely place for a world-renowned drug treatment center, but that is the home of Hazelden. This forty-year-old rehabilitation program, known for its trend-setting, comprehensive approach to treating drug and alcohol addiction, has earned a reputation as a leader in the field of drug treatment services.

The story of Hazelden is impressive, partly because of its huge scale of operations. In addition to the sprawling campus in Center City, Minnesota, Hazelden operates facilities in Minneapolis, St. Paul, and Plymouth, Minnesota; Irving, Texas; West Palm Beach, Florida; and Detroit, Michigan. The organization operates a publications distribution center in Cork, Ireland, and plans are under way to start a new Hazelden facility in the northeastern United States. Hazelden employs more than 900 people, ranging from counselors and registered nurses to psychologists and clergy. Its rehabilitation services include a standard residential program, an extended rehabilitation program, aftercare services, a family center, a women's program, an adolescent and young adult program, a residential intermediate care facility, retreat services, and outpatient treatment. Hazelden also offers training for chemical dependency counselors, clinical-pastoral education, and health promotion services for businesses, government, schools and colleges, and community groups. Its publishing operation is said to be the world's largest publisher of self-help literature.

The breadth of Hazelden's services is certainly extraordinary, but employees stress that the extensive services are essential elements in the so-called Minnesota Model. This famous philosophy of drug and alcohol rehabilitation relies on the team approach: a multidisciplinary treatment staff assesses the problems of each individual patient, taking into consideration not only chemical dependency but also family situations, physical health, social and economic status, spiritual beliefs, and so on. According to this model, all these areas of a patient's life are affected by drug abuse and each must be dealt with in relation to the others. This style of rehabilitation, which has become the most widely adopted drug treatment strategy in the United States, allows the patient to reconstruct the many pieces of his or her life that have been shattered by drug abuse.

Other rehabilitation philosophies have been structured to identify a reason for chemical dependency, "cure" it, and then return the person to "normal" living. That approach does not necessarily work too well, according to Hazelden counselors, because most serious drug dependency situations are so complicated that there really is no single cure to be offered. In such circumstances, the addicted individual primarily needs to be supported, reassured that his condition is not something to feel guilty about, and instructed in effective ways to cope with dependency.

"The philosophy at Hazelden is that alcoholism and chemical dependency is a 'no fault' illness or condition," one Hazelden counselor explains. "We've found that searching for a cause isn't necessarily productive. A lot of time and energy can be lost looking for the cause when it's really more important to be working toward a realistic solution."

Started in 1949 as a rehabilitation center for alcoholic professionals from the Twin Cities area of Minnesota, Hazelden has gradually evolved into a facility that accepts people of any background. Today, the Twelve Steps of Alcoholics Anonymous (A.A.) form the foundation of all of Hazelden's rehabilitation programs. The stated goal for all those in treatment is total abstinence from alcohol and other drugs.

The cost of the average thirty-day primary rehabilitation program, which includes at least twenty-four hours of close medical monitoring and/or detoxification, group therapy, individual counseling, lectures, and other therapies, is approximately $6,000. Charges may vary depending on the patient's desire for private or semi-private accommodations, specialized medical needs, books, and other miscellaneous items.

RESIDENTIAL PRIMARY REHABILITATION PROGRAM

The backbone of Hazelden, Residential Primary Rehabilitation, served a record 1,706 people in 1988. About 80 percent of these individuals came from outside Minnesota. Many were self-referred while others were referred by families, friends, the legal system, churches, or other interested parties.

The first step in the primary rehabilitation program is detoxification, if necessary. In general, the purpose of detoxification is to remove toxic substances (drugs or alcohol) from the body. Upon entering the Hazelden program, all patients spend twenty-four hours in the Medical Skilled Unit where they undergo complete physical examinations to assess their general health and level of chemical dependency. Depending on the drugs used by the addict and the level of addiction, detoxification can be as basic as a regimen of proper nutrition and the opportunity for sleep, or as thorough as a physician-directed medication program.

Patients suffering from serious addictions, including alcohol dependency, are likely to experience severe, even life-threatening, withdrawal symptoms. These symptoms are liable to include convulsions or seizures, hallucinations, and mental confusion. Health care professionals are able to treat some of these conditions with medications that reduce the symptoms and make the patient somewhat more comfortable. Gradually, physician-ordered medications can be tapered off until the patient is completely drug-free. Then, with the toxic substances removed, it is possible to begin treatment.

After detoxification, patients in the primary rehabilitation program report to one of six therapy units at the Center City campus. Each 128-bed unit is fully equipped for the patient's stay—there are bedrooms, laundry facilities, refrigerators, lounges, meeting rooms, and so on. Men and women are lodged separately and generally do not mingle during treatment.

To plan the appropriate treatment schedule, a team of chemical dependency counselors, medical professionals, clergy, and recreational therapists conducts a thorough assessment of the patient. Based on interviews with the patient and his or her history of substance abuse, the rehabilitation plan sets specific goals for the various areas of the patient's life.

"The first part of an individualized treatment program is a complete assessment," explains Mike Schiks, director of Hazelden's adolescent treatment program, which is based on the principles of the primary rehabilitation program. "Twenty questions just doesn't do it. Using the multidisciplinary approach, we have a team of professionals from different fields interview the patient and make an independent assessment. Then the individual assessments are pooled and a treatment plan is set up."

For about thirty days, the patient is immersed in the treatment program—daily lectures and presentations by a range of health professionals provide extensive education on the subject of substance abuse, daily group therapy sessions provide support and offer opportunities to share personal experiences. These group sessions are designed to build trust and confidence. Separate individual counseling with an assigned therapist helps the patient to focus on the unique personal issues and experiences related to his or her own drug abuse.

The highly structured environment of this residential rehabilitation program is purposeful. Since most addicts have rejected anything even resembling a schedule, learning to live with structure is an important step toward rehabilitation. However, such structure can meet resistance from patients. The key to overcoming these obstacles, according to Schiks, is in the presentation of the structure to the patient.

"You can present the structure in one of two ways," he says. "You can say 'These are the rules and you are going to follow them.' Or you can say, 'We believe you are a capable person and while you are here we think you are capable of following some basic rules, don't you?'

"The first approach is the 'rules' method, which sets the stage for a power struggle between staff and those in treatment. The second approach is what we call the 'expectation' approach where patients are asked to live up to certain expectations. The expectation approach empowers the person in treatment— the person in treatment is making a choice and participating in his own recovery. Empowerment is what we want them to take with them when they leave here."

While the primary rehabilitation program is usually completed in about one month, aftercare— counseling and support after treatment—continues indefinitely. Aftercare stems from the realization that true recovery from chemical dependency is more than just living a drug-free life-style. It involves on-going efforts to refrain from drug use while attempting to replace it with more healthy practices, such as good relationships and self-help efforts. Through aftercare and support groups, problems that linger after completion of primary rehabilitation can be dealt with on a long-term basis.

OTHER HAZELDEN REHABILITATION SERVICES

Hazelden Family Programs

At the same time as the Hazelden patient is undergoing primary therapy, family members or others closely involved in the patient's life may participate in a special program on the Center City campus to assist their own recovery and adjustment. The five- to seven-day program at the Hazelden Family Center was initiated to help those living with chemically dependent individuals, many of whom are or have been chemically dependent themselves. Problems such as physical and psychological abuse, economic difficulties, and lingering hostilities and resentments are common situations in families touched by drug abuse. The Family Center offers strategies to deal with these situations.

52

Similarly, Hazelden Family Forums are weekly educational and supportive programs held in Minneapolis for family and friends of chemically dependent individuals. The six-week program is similar to that of the Hazelden Family Center, but is offered as a type of outpatient arrangement.

The growing awareness of the impact of drug abuse on the family and friends of addicts has led to some new and expanded approaches to drug treatment. Programs like the Hazelden Family Center and Family Forums reflect these new developments. For example, both programs utilize the principles of Al-Anon, a self-help organization based on A.A. ideals that focuses on the problems of people close to drug abusers, the so-called "secondary victims." Al-Anon and similar groups spring from a relatively new concept known as *codependency*, which is the theory that when people are part of a group (such as a family) which is experiencing unusual emotional strain (such as drug or alcohol abuse), they often develop unhealthy behaviors themselves. In the case of a teenager who becomes drug dependent, his parents or siblings might react to the situation in any number of unhealthy ways. They may become perfectionists or "workaholics," they may lose their self-confidence, or develop addictions of their own—all in an effort to survive in the destructive environment created by the teen's addiction. These types of secondary problems, although directly related to a single individual's chemical dependency, are really separate issues that need to be treated independently.

The intense atmosphere of primary rehabilitation can leave a patient drained. Having accepted his powerlessness over addiction, faced up to the pain and suffering he has caused himself and the people closest to him, and pledged to live a drug-free life, it

53

is not uncommon for the patient to feel vulnerable and afraid. Under such circumstances, the reality of starting life over can be very intimidating.

For this very reason, the Hazelden Fellowship Club, a halfway house in St. Paul, opens its doors to those trying to make the transition from primary treatment to independent living in the community. This fifty-five-bed intermediate care facility serves both men and women, ages eighteen to sixty-five. There is a $62 per day charge for residents. The environment at Fellowship Club is both structured and supportive, a place where residents can practice and master the many skills needed to live independently. Residents are expected to do household chores, make their bed, and attend breakfast daily. Chemical dependency counselors and clergy continue to provide guidance through counseling sessions, and residents also participate in peer groups and hold outside jobs. On average, residents stay at Fellowship Club for three to five months before returning to the community on their own.

Hazelden touts Fellowship Club as an important step toward long-term health for those struggling to overcome chemical dependency. According to Hazelden statistics, 61 percent of Fellowship Club residents have abstained from drugs and alcohol one year after leaving the halfway house. Sixty-seven percent report improved relationships and 94 percent claim to have had improvement in the overall quality of their lives. Such figures compare very favorably to other treatment programs.

Perhaps the breadth of Hazelden's outreach is most apparent in the specialized programs set up for the unique needs of certain groups of chemically dependent persons. The Hazelden Pioneer House in Plymouth, Minnesota, and the Women's Program in

Minneapolis are just two of the programs established with special functions in mind.

Pioneer House is a sixty-four-bed residential treatment facility for adolescents and young adults (and their families). Located on the shores of Medicine Lake, Pioneer House is structured along the same lines as the primary rehabilitation program at the Center City campus, but therapy is geared toward the special educational, developmental, and recreational requirements of young persons, aged fourteen to twenty-five. For instance, instructors at Pioneer House contact the patient's home school district and design an educational program to continue his or her learning at the appropriate level. There are also screening and referral services for patients' learning disabilities or vocational problems. The average stay at Pioneer House is about six weeks.

"At the heart of treatment is the need to be treated with respect and dignity," says counselor Mike Schiks. "That's especially important to young people as they carve out their personality. They need to be validated and reassured that they and their opinions are valued.

"Some time in the 1970s, a confrontive style of treatment developed and that has tended to hang on longer with programs treating adolescents. But we reject that model. We believe that if people are presented with information about their condition in a way they can understand, most often they'll change or at least investigate change."

Presenting information about chemical dependency in a way that can be readily understood by adolescents requires counselors to translate abstract, theoretical literature into more down-to-earth language. In addition, approaches geared toward adolescent addicts are emphasized, including peer groups and participatory programs such as patient government.

"When they are involved in the process of their own recovery, they're more likely to respond to our input," Schiks says.

The Women's Program in Minneapolis is an outpatient program that began a decade ago in response to the special needs of women completing conventional rehabilitation programs. As noted earlier, many of these programs were based on confrontational techniques designed to shock or alarm addicts into the recovery process. However, most such programs were geared toward men and the "rehabilitation" experience was often nothing less than traumatic. For women, who usually respond better to less hostile rehabilitation methods, participation in these confrontational programs often led to further emotional problems. The Hazelden Women's Program set out to remedy this situation by providing a more supportive environment for rehabilitation.

"The most important thing we want to do is to provide a place where women can feel safe," says Elizabeth Farrell, a supervisor/counselor at the Women's Program. "Within everyone there's a little child and we try to work with that part of the people we see. Addictions are an extension of the frightened child within people. Because they don't feel safe for one reason or another, addiction is the response."

The treatment offered at the Hazelden Women's Program also parallels the primary rehabilitation program at Center City, taking into account the special problems likely to be encountered by women drug addicts. One such problem is the fact that many women today are single heads of households, which makes treatment of their chemical dependency problems more difficult and, many say, more important. Often a four- or six-week visit to a residential drug rehabilitation facility is out of the question. Such programs are, by design, much more expensive, and even if financing could be arranged, it is unlikely that a single mother would be willing or able to be separated from her children for a month or more. When rehabilitation is made accessible on an outpatient basis during the day and evening hours, many women can take advantage of therapy while continuing their responsibilities at home and at work.

Furthermore, outpatient rehabilitation offers a certain measure of privacy that is not possible with residential treatment. Women seeking outpatient treatment can continue to live near-normal lives without announcing their addiction by having to go away for an extended period of residential rehabilitation. This, too, is an important consideration for many people.

The Women's Program consists of five weeks of primary rehabilitation followed by ten weeks of aftercare. In the primary treatment phase, participants meet for three hours three times per week. Through intensive group therapy, the Twelve Steps, and other recovery resources, Farrell says, the women are encouraged to explore their inner selves. By looking inward, it is hoped that the women can "tap into" sources of strength that will help them overcome their chemical dependency. At the same time, the primary treatment phase is full of opportunities for the women to build personal relationships with other women in the program. Often, meaningful friendships with other women are lacking among those who enter the Women's Program. It is hoped that these experiences will foster strong ties within the group—ties that will aid recovery. Counselors in the Women's Program say this "spiritual" approach to the problem of chemical dependency is powerful and effective.

"We help them get beyond words about recovery to a deeper understanding of themselves and their dependency problems," Farrell states. "That's where real recovery can be found."

In the aftercare phase, skills learned in primary treatment are put into practice. Attendance at the Women's Program center is cut back to once a week and participation in an outside aftercare program like A.A. is required. During this ten-week phase, their formal rehabilitation program becomes less intensive, but participants must develop a support system that will assist their long-term recovery. In addition to involvement in A.A.-type groups, cultivation of the support system can mean rebuilding family relationships, if possible.

SHAPING NATIONAL PRIORITIES

In an effort to further drug and alcohol dependency treatment and prevention nationwide, Hazelden uses its position of leadership in the field to raise issues it considers to be important. For instance, the organization is currently working to redirect national priorities in the antidrug effort. Stated Hazelden Foundation President Harold A. Swift in a recent review:

> The "War on Drugs" continues to ignore alcohol as our number one drug problem. And, it continues to focus on enforcement and interdiction (interruption of supply) rather than on prevention, education and treatment to change our cultural attitudes about alcohol and other drug use.

The criticisms seem to have some validity. As noted, the human and economic devastation brought about by alcoholism in the United States far exceeds that associated with cocaine and other "hard" drugs. Furthermore, the portrayal of alcohol use as a natural part of the American way of life—particularly the promotion of alcohol in advertisements geared toward young people—threatens to extend this aspect of the U.S. drug problem well into the future. The nation's much publicized "War on Drugs" also leaves many in the drug treatment and prevention communities with little optimism since less than one-third of the antidrug effort is geared toward treatment and prevention programs.

With these obstacles, the campaign against drug dependency is rightly viewed as an uphill battle by those involved in rehabilitation efforts. Even in a more supportive environment, they concede, there would still be enormous societal problems (economic hardship, the breakdown of the traditional family, educational deficiencies, and so on) that would continue to promote drug and alcohol dependency. Ingrained cultural attitudes and inadequate funding of treatment programs only make the job of reducing drug abuse and dependency that much more difficult.

Nevertheless, comprehensive residential and outpatient rehabilitation programs represent a glimmer of hope that the complex problems associated with drugs and alcohol can be dealt with effectively.

CHAPTER FOUR
METHADONE MAINTENANCE TREATMENT

Throughout the long American effort to deal with the problem of drug addiction, various innovations have come along that promised success. In the first decade of this century, lawmakers made their initial attempts to curtail the importation of addictive substances into the United States. By the 1920s, municipal governments established "narcotics clinics," which dispensed cocaine, morphine, and heroin to local addicts. The clinics' goals varied: some sought eventual abstinence while others were contented with indefinite maintenance. Later, therapeutic communities designed to make addicts come to terms with underlying emotional and physical problems emerged. Other groups advocated novel treatment philosophies as well. However, no innovation in the struggle against illegal drug use has been quite so radical nor quite so controversial as the concept of methadone maintenance for heroin addiction.

Developed in 1965 by New York researchers Marie Nyswander and Vincent Dole, methadone maintenance has remained a hotly debated topic throughout its history. Today, the debate persists with advocates and critics clashing over a whole range of issues, from whether methadone maintenance treatment works to whether it is proper. The debate over this particular treatment approach is interesting not only because methadone maintenance is one of the primary drug treatment options, but also because it highlights a host of other topics, including the role of methadone in AIDS prevention and the propriety of governmental involvement in the distribution of addictive substances.

Methadone maintenance treatment is drug replacement therapy. To reduce the dangerous practice of injecting heroin with needles, addicts in these programs visit a clinic where they are given *methadone hydrochloride*, a human-made painkilling drug. The bitter-tasting methadone tablet is usually dissolved in liquid (frequently orange juice) and the patient drinks it down. Unlike the heroin it replaces, methadone produces little or no euphoria, yet it satisfies the heroin addict's physical dependence on opiates. Furthermore, methadone blocks the euphoric effects of heroin, which tends to discourage continued heroin use.

Methadone is a long-acting drug; a properly adjusted dosage is effective for twenty-four to thirty-six hours. In contrast, the short-lived effect of heroin means addicts must "shoot up" four or five times a day to sustain a high. Proponents of methadone maintenance point out that because it is longer-acting, methadone frees heroin addicts from the endless search for another "fix" and allows them to concentrate on more productive pursuits like holding a job, caring for their children, and working toward recovery.

Since methadone is an addictive substance, its

use is strictly controlled by federal and state regulations. Methadone clinics, staffed with physicians, nurses, and other medical professionals, must perform regular examinations (urine testing and general observation, most commonly) to certify that their clients are not using any other illegal drugs. Some clinics limit the length of time patients can receive methadone or set maximum dose levels that can be prescribed. Clinics also have policies governing "take-home" methadone, which determine whether patients can take supplies of the drug from the clinic for weekends, holidays, or out-of-town trips. All these regulations are intended to carefully manage the use of this substance and keep it from becoming another street drug.

In addition to dispensing methadone, these clinics also have a staff of professional drug counselors who oversee the individualized care of each patient. Once patients have been stabilized by methadone, the counselors engage in psychotherapy as well as general counseling about drug abuse. These counseling services are intended to complement the administration of methadone and ensure the broader rehabilitation of patients. Medical attention for the health problems that usually accompany IV-drug use is also provided and, in some cases, vocational and educational services are available. Once accepted into a methadone maintenance program, patients are expected to adhere to a daily attendance schedule, cooperate with clinic personnel, find a job or enroll in school, and abstain from illegal drug use.

It is important to realize that methadone alone is not necessarily a bridge to drug-free living; in fact, some patients claim methadone addiction is more powerful than heroin. For this reason, critics denounce it as a crutch, a legalized form of drug addiction, or even a devious government-backed plan to keep drug addicts "doped up." The methadone patient has, these critics say, simply exchanged the heroin addiction for a methadone addiction. Technically, this is true. A patient following a methadone maintenance program literally substitutes one drug habit for another. Methadone advocates admit this fact, but counter that methadone is a safer substance that permits heroin addicts to live more stable, socially acceptable lives than is possible with continued opiate dependency.

The controversies surrounding methadone start with the goals of this type of drug treatment. Unlike many other forms of treatment, most methadone clinics do not push their patients to achieve complete abstinence from drugs.[1] Instead, the primary objective of most methadone treatment centers is the elimination of heroin use and the rehabilitation of heroin addicts. Abstinence, however, is at the heart of a great many other treatment approaches, including the Twelve Steps approach developed by Alcoholics Anonymous. This philosophical difference has occasionally led to serious splits between those involved in methadone maintenance and those in other areas of the drug treatment community.

The rationale behind methadone treatment is the theory that many or all opiate addicts suffer from a physical imbalance that drives them to the use of opiate drugs. This internal imbalance makes it difficult or impossible for such individuals to function without opiates. Furthermore, according to this theory, addiction is a chronic or lifelong condition that can be treated, but never cured. Accepting this unpleasant diagnosis, methadone clinics attempt to provide medical therapy (methadone) for a specific physical condition (heroin dependency), just as a doctor prescribes insulin for diabetes.

The notion that a physical imbalance is the reason behind addiction has gained widespread acceptance in the medical community. Most health professionals today agree that opiate dependency is rooted in physical factors. (The question of whether the physical imbalance existed before addiction or was actually created by addiction, however, remains a topic of debate.) Despite medical explanations, there is still a belief among many people, including many addicts and counselors, that drug addiction represents a sort of moral failure or weakness of character. Such "moral" explanations of drug dependency tend to run strongly against methadone maintenance treatment for the very reason that methadone patients continue to depend on an addictive substance.

However, methadone clinics' efforts to reduce heroin use and rehabilitate heroin addicts have achieved considerable success. Scientific studies have shown that nearly three-fourths of heroin addicts who participate in methadone maintenance programs for two years stop injecting heroin. Moreover, studies indicate that the use of other drugs decreases the longer addicts stick with the methadone treatment program. Also of major importance is the fact that continued methadone maintenance is associated with reduced criminal activity of addicts; without the physical need for heroin, addicts are less inclined to commit crimes to support their expensive drug habit. Such positive developments are all necessary steps in rehabilitation. To professionals involved in methadone maintenance, these developments represent success in the areas of major concern.

"I have clients who say they've done everything to stop using heroin, but couldn't do it," says Gretchen Blais, a counselor at the 14th Street Clinic in Oakland, California. "Methadone is the one thing that's allowed them to stop using. With it, they're able to get their lives together and get into recovery. They couldn't get there any other way."

CHART 3

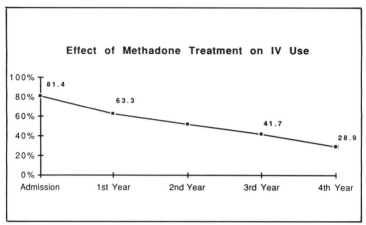

Research indicates that continued participation in a methadone maintenance program gradually reduces intravenous (IV) drug use. The chart above, displaying data collected by researchers at the National Institute on Drug Abuse, shows the steady decline in IV drug use among 388 men over a period of four years. At the time of admission to a methadone maintenance program, 81.4% of the study subjects were injecting drugs intravenously. (The remaining 18.6% came to the methadone program after a period of imprisonment or completion of another drug treatment program and were not classified as active IV drug users.) Over the course of the study, IV drug use was reduced by 71%.

(Ball, JC, et al.: Journal of Health and Social Behavior 29:214–226, 1988.)

CONTINUING CONTROVERSIES

It would be inaccurate to imply that the controversies over methadone begin and end with the "moral" argument about dispensing addictive substances to known addicts. Actually, there are other issues to be considered as well. Among them:

- wide variations in quality from one methadone program to the next
- establishing proper dosages for methadone patients
- preventing methadone from becoming another addictive substance for law enforcement authorities to battle

The success of methadone treatment varies dramatically from program to program. A well-run clinic requires adequate funding and capable administrators who can wade through the many regulations governing the use of methadone. Trained health professionals are needed to provide physical examinations and the appropriate methadone doses to patients (a critically important factor in methadone maintenance), while counselors and psychiatrists at the clinic must help addicts deal with their emotional and psychological problems. With such material and human resources, clinics can achieve impressive levels of success.

Unfortunately, most methadone clinics are not so lucky. Chronically short of money and qualified staff, they are frequently located in dilapidated inner city neighborhoods. This environmental handicap often breeds failure, according to many methadone experts. Surrounded by unemployment, crime, and the easy availability of other drugs like cocaine and alcohol, these methadone clinics are limited in what they can offer patients. However, the negative stigma often associated with methadone patients can keep the centers from opening in more desirable areas.

Another important variable influencing the quality of a methadone clinic is staff continuity. High turnover rates among staff members lead to a breakdown in the all-important relationship between counselor and client. The most effective methadone programs are built on the personal ties that keep patients coming back day in and day out for their medication. Without that personal touch, effectiveness drops off dramatically.

Finally, it is important that patients in methadone maintenance programs be actively involved in designing and carrying out their own treatment plan. As treatment progresses, adjustments in dosages and patient behavior are necessary. It is an essential part of the rehabilitation process for patients to be involved in the decision making. In fact, federal regulations require patient involvement in the design and updating of the methadone treatment plan, but many studies show that does not occur.

Within the methadone maintenance community, one of the most hotly debated topics relating to this form of drug treatment is the issue of doses. How high a dose of methadone is needed to satisfy the opiate addict's craving and, thus, discourage the use of illegal heroin? Who should set the dose? There is a wide variety of opinion on these questions and it is not uncommon for politics to be dragged into the argument.

Today, methadone doses vary from one clinic to the next, according to federal and state laws as well as the clinics' own policies. Typically, doses range from less than 10 milligrams (mg) to in excess of 100 mg per day. Usually, doses are highest during the early phases of treatment and then are gradually reduced to the lowest level needed to satisfy the individual addict's need.

The level at which methadone adequately controls opiate craving is called the "blocking dose." As with other medications, however, the same dose is liable to produce very different results in different people. Thus, the blocking dose varies widely. If the level is inadequate, opiate addicts will experience withdrawal symptoms and will likely seek out their former drug of choice—heroin—or other illegal drugs.

With these variables, disputes over dose levels are relatively frequent. In general, professionals in the methadone maintenance field contend that rather than dispensing methadone solely according to government standards, clinics should set doses according to individual needs.

In a broader context, some methadone advocates also believe that prevailing social pressures against methadone maintenance have generally kept doses too low. As a result, methadone patients, being inadequately medicated, return to illegal drug use. This, in turn, casts doubt on the effectiveness of methadone maintenance and perpetuates the bias against this method of treatment.

Since the inception of methadone maintenance programs, the prospect of *diversion*, or the illegal sale of methadone as a street drug, has remained a troublesome problem. Law enforcement authorities, already overwhelmed by illegal drug trafficking, are justifiably concerned that methadone may add to their difficulties.

Mostly, diversion occurs as a result of some patients' abuse of take-home privileges. Given a certain quantity of methadone to last through a weekend or holiday, some patients choose to sell their dose on the street rather than take it themselves. Robberies of methadone clinics also release the drug onto the streets from time to time. And, in yet another method of diversion, it is not unheard of for patients to hold their daily methadone dose in their mouths, avoid swallowing, spit it out after leaving the clinic, and then sell it to someone else. To combat this last diversion technique, the 14th Street Clinic in Oakland has set up a test.

"They (patients) must take the dose, say thank

you to the nurse, and then drink some water afterward," explains Gretchen Blais. "It's kind of hard to say thank you when your mouth is full!"

Most clinic personnel view diversion as an unavoidable predicament, but not one that is adding significantly to the nation's drug problems. Politically, the problem of diversion hurts the reputation of methadone maintenance programs, but even the federal Drug Enforcement Agency does not consider it a grave threat.

THE URGENT PROBLEM OF AIDS

Since the mid-1980s, it has become obvious that the United States and the world face a serious public health dilemma in the form of the acquired immune deficiency syndrome (AIDS) epidemic. This virus has already taken the lives of a hundred thousand Americans and infection rates are rising every year. Despite massive research efforts, vaccines and cures still remain elusive. The potential long-term consequences of this epidemic are alarming, in both human and economic costs.

Intravenous (IV)-drug users, notably heroin addicts, are a growing segment of the AIDS population because of their practice of sharing needles. It is estimated that more than half of the IV-drug user population in New York City carries the AIDS virus. Furthermore, IV-drug users are the primary transmitters of the AIDS virus to the heterosexual and infant populations. Faced with the growing dimensions of the disease and the prominent role IV-drug users play in its spread, health officials are trying to develop strategies to control future transmission. Drug treatment programs in general, and methadone clinics in particular, are touted by many as an important part of the response to the AIDS epidemic because of their potential for reducing IV-drug use and needle sharing.

Discussing the potential consequences of the AIDS epidemic and possible strategies to deal with it, Dr. James R. Cooper of the National Institute on Drug Abuse concluded:

> *The most important health objectives will be to attract intravenous opiate users into treatment early in their addiction careers, stop their intravenous drug use and sharing of injection equipment, and retain them in treatment. Preliminary data support the abundant existing evidence that many intravenous opiate users stop injecting drugs when adequate doses of methadone are given and suggest that methadone treatment has a critical role to play in curtailing the spread of AIDS."[2]*

Unlike the confrontational techniques employed in some treatment programs, the philosophy guiding methadone maintenance is basically one of support and patience. Heroin addicts are viewed as individuals with terrific problems—problems that could lead to their demise without the assistance of methadone. Working within the context of a maintenance program, it may be natural for counselors at methadone clinics to take an uncommonly long view of the recovery process and, possibly, grant some extra leeway to their troubled patients.

"At this clinic, we don't kick them out for dirty (drug-tainted) urines," says Blais of the 14th Street Clinic. "Research has shown that with increasing length of treatment comes higher probability of recovery.

"Right now I'm working with an addict who's

71

CHART 4

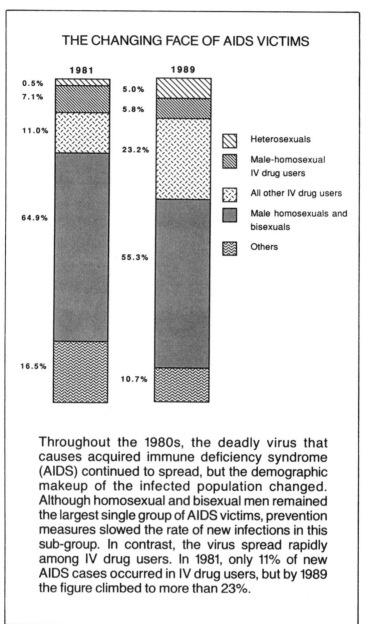

THE CHANGING FACE OF AIDS VICTIMS

1981   1989

0.5%
7.1%
5.0%
5.8%

11.0%
23.2%

Heterosexuals

Male-homosexual
IV drug users

All other IV drug users

Male homosexuals and
bisexuals

Others

64.9%

55.3%

16.5%
10.7%

Throughout the 1980s, the deadly virus that
causes acquired immune deficiency syndrome
(AIDS) continued to spread, but the demographic
makeup of the infected population changed.
Although homosexual and bisexual men remained
the largest single group of AIDS victims, prevention
measures slowed the rate of new infections in this
sub-group. In contrast, the virus spread rapidly
among IV drug users. In 1981, only 11% of new
AIDS cases occurred in IV drug users, but by 1989
the figure climbed to more than 23%.

been addicted to drugs since she was about sixteen. She's thirty-six now. She's lived the kind of life that could have landed her in jail. She could have been dead. But she's stayed with the methadone program for three years now. And it's just in the past year that she's started to come around. I think she's made her mind up to recover."

CHAPTER FIVE
SPECIAL NEEDS OF THE ADOLESCENT DRUG ADDICT

"I hate you and I hate this place!"

The words caromed down the hallway. The statement didn't seem to be the product of much reflection. As a matter of fact, it was screamed in the midst of a heated argument. Before the final syllable had faded, a teenaged guy darted out of a doorway and walked quickly toward me.

"Everybody who works here is full of it," he informed me. "Don't believe anything they say."

"OK," I said as he rushed by and stomped down a flight of stairs leading to the basement.

A moment later, a young woman emerged from the same office down the hall, following in leisurely pursuit of the blond-haired youth. As she passed, she hesitated slightly and said, "I'll be with you in a minute, OK?" She continued on down the stairs.

It's another day at Woodlands Treatment Center, an adolescent residential drug rehabilitation facility in Burlington, Iowa. Actually, it isn't just *any* other day—it's Family Day. This is when families and clients spend some time together at the treatment center or arrange for a pass so they can go elsewhere for a short period. Naturally, emotions run high on such occasions. Many times, clients are upset by family members' arrival; just as often, however, there is resentment over a no-show.

Julie Warden, the Woodlands counselor involved in this particular argument, returned shortly and apologized for the outburst.

"It's one of those days," she explained. "He's mad at me because I wouldn't give him a pass on short notice. We have rules that clients need to follow to get permission to leave. He came to me this morning and told me he wanted a pass and I didn't give it to him. So he's mad.

"It won't be long before we hear his stereo blaring, 'You've Got to Fight for Your Right to Party,'" she says with some amount of resignation. "That's OK. Dealing with anger is one of the most common things we do here. We'll talk about it later when he calms down."

Woodlands Treatment Center, nestled beside a quiet road on the outskirts of town, is one of only two treatment facilities in the state of Iowa to specialize in the rehabilitation of adolescent addicts. Consequently, the utilization rate at the ten-bed, boys-only facility is consistently high. Presently, only court-ordered clients are accepted.

The center began operations in 1986 under the auspices of Young House Family Services, Incorporated, a local Christian agency serving young people and their families. Since its inception, Woodlands has grown steadily and today the center employs ten full-time and five part-time staff counselors. In addition, there are plans to build another wing at the facility to accommodate adolescent girls. The need for Woodlands' expansion is pressing, even in a sparsely populated, rural state like Iowa. Because its adolescent treatment program is almost unique in the state and because an ever-increasing number of young drug abusers are in need of treatment, the center appears to be headed toward a busy future.

"This is the type of job that you'd be thrilled if the need died, but that's not what's happening," says Warden. "In fact, it's just the opposite. The need is growing faster than we can deal with."

TREATING THE ADOLESCENT DRUG ADDICT

Perhaps the type of heated exchange between staff and client described earlier is standard fare at many drug rehabilitation centers, but there are some basic differences between the treatment of young drug addicts and their adult counterparts. According to the professional counselors at Woodlands, among the biggest factors to be considered in the treatment of adolescents are the many unique developmental needs of younger people. These needs frequently include: overcoming childhood problems and developing a strong identity; dealing with the specific implications of addiction rather than discussing abstract ideas; achieving emotional maturity; and confronting the seriousness of their drug problem.

"The energy level of adolescents is incredible," Julie Warden says. "And within that energy level, you have their hormonal imbalances. These kids are changing in a lot of different ways. Their sexual identity is being developed at this time in their lives and that is a difficult thing to handle for many of them. It's a difficult thing for many clean people to handle; being dependent on drugs only makes it worse."

The problem of establishing one's identity is compounded by the fact that a great many adolescent substance abusers suffer from a past that includes parental neglect or sexual abuse. At one point eight of the ten adolescents in the Woodlands treatment program were victims of sexual abuse, according to Sandy Andre-Krell, director of Woodlands. Such children typically experience a range of developmental problems, including difficulty building strong relationships (particularly with peers), low self-esteem, and lack of positive role models. Treatment programs for young people need to address these specific problem areas and teach the basic personal skills needed to overcome them.

Part of the solution appears to be the imposition of a highly structured environment. While this tool is also employed in many adult treatment programs, most professionals emphasize that the need for structure is particularly important for adolescents. Often these young people have never experienced stability or structure at any time in their entire lives: they may come from broken homes where one or both parents neglected their responsibilities; they may have dropped out of school or been expelled; if they stayed in school, they may have made a habit of cutting classes. Successful recovery from drug dependency requires that they incorporate some type of constructive structure into their lives—steady employment, regular attendance at school, or long-term relationships based on trust and honesty. Since such a life-style is usually completely foreign to these adolescents, it must be taught and practiced in the treatment program.

"An important aspect of the treatment program is just keeping them occupied with activities," explains Andre-Krell. "They are up at 6:45 A.M. and from that time until they go to bed at about 10:30 P.M., there's no more than one-half hour of free time. They take fifteen-minute breaks between activities like classes or therapy groups, but that's it.

"For nearly all of the kids who come here, it's a very new experience to not have large blocks of time where they can do whatever they feel like doing, which in their cases has usually been drugs and alcohol. Getting away from that life-style means adopting a new one that forces them to set schedules for themselves."

Structure comes in other forms as well. Rules govern the consumption of food (meals are to be eaten in the dining area only, all clients are expected to remain in the dining area for a minimum of twenty minutes at each meal, eating is allowed only after everyone is served, sugar intake is limited, etc.) and proper attire (all shirts must be buttoned to the top of the chest, no hats or sunglasses may be worn inside, shorts may be worn only if it is 75 degrees or more outside, all shorts must have at least 4-inch inseams, etc.). In addition, there are detailed guidelines relating to the upkeep of the facility, curfews, gambling, obscene language, music, relationships, tobacco use, telephone time, and sick days. These and other rules are all part of the effort to promote the positive qualities of discipline and adherence to schedules.

"I'd say that the kids who have the most success after leaving here are the ones who establish some type of positive structure in their own lives," Andre-Krell observes.

Focusing on Specifics

The developmental level of the adolescent drug addict also dictates the use of appropriate learning resources. Books, assignments, and presentations used in the rehabilitation program are not philosophical or abstract; rather they are geared toward very specific areas of the client's life that need improvement. For instance, in the early stages of the treatment program (known as the Intake Phase), each client must complete a list of at least "50 Insanities" and "50 Interferences." The insanities list details of reckless acts committed under the influence of drugs and is intended to teach clients how they have participated in the creation of their own problems. A typical insanities list will include behavior such as driving while intoxicated, playing "chicken," lying, using drugs at school, or cutting classes. The interferences list, which is used to demonstrate how the client's drug use has adversely affected others, usually includes things like stealing, hurting friends and family, threatening pedestrians or other motorists, and damaging others' property.

"All the documents we use in the treatment of adolescents are more concrete than those used in adult programs," explains Andre-Krell. "In addition, the reading level of our materials is much lower. About third or fourth grade, usually."

That brings up yet another point about the typical adolescent drug abuser's developmental level. These clients are usually educationally deficient. For many, drug use has resulted in their dropping out of school or being expelled. Others have missed a great many school days. Individual educational deficiency depends on the severity and length of drug abuse. While some of the clients at Woodlands may exceed the third or fourth grade reading level, most are at least one to two years behind others their age in school.

To prevent any further educational backsliding while residents are in treatment, a teacher from the local public school system visits Woodlands for two and a half to four hours every day throughout the year. The teacher contacts home school districts to determine each resident's educational background and begins instruction at the appropriate level. Residents are expected to take responsibility for their education and won't graduate from Woodlands without continued scholastic progress throughout treatment.

Another unique aspect of treatment for young addicts involves teaching them—usually, from scratch—how to deal with normal human emotions in healthy and constructive ways. Often, the teaching process includes thorough lessons on topics such as honesty, anger, and self-image. Throughout the treatment program, clients are required to complete various assignments (reading, writing, role playing) designed to make them confront the range of feelings they are likely to experience in the course of their lives. Often, however, the lessons on dealing with feelings aren't taught out of a book or in a group therapy session.

"Today, we have a couple of kids who are on room assignments, which means they can't leave their rooms," Andre-Krell explained on one visit. "They didn't want to participate in some of the planned activities, which is fine, but if they don't want to take part then they have to stay in their rooms. Those are the rules.

"The story behind one of the guys is that he just had a rip-roaring argument with his dad and, although he won't admit it, he's hurting and he's angry. He's been slamming doors and blasting his music, but that's tapering off in the past day or so. He's getting over it slowly and that's good. Maybe next time he'll only be mad for one day, and the time after that just a few hours. Eventually, maybe he'll see that the best way to deal with his anger and hurt is to talk with someone about it, rather than refusing to participate in things. That's what we're shooting for.

"It's a real hard process, though. What we're really doing here is more *habilitation* than rehabilitation. We're starting from scratch with a lot of kids. They've never learned how to respond to their feelings in a constructive manner, so it's not just a matter of reminding them of things they already know. It's a matter of teaching them for the very first time what to do in these situations."

In addition to being a supportive and educational setting, an adolescent rehabilitation facility must also confront the young people about their lifestyle and challenge them to make a change. This can be a difficult balance to achieve and it is another reason why treatment programs designed specifically for adolescents are so important. Often, when younger drug addicts enter rehabilitation at an adult treatment center the counseling staff and the other clients are reluctant to make the youngsters fully responsible for their behavior. Thus, young drug addicts frequently fail to face up to the seriousness of their drug problems.

"One hazard of putting adolescents in adult programs is they can fool adults into thinking they're innocent little kids," Warden explains. "Often, the feeling is, 'Oh, they couldn't have done anything so bad. They're just little kids.' In that setting, young people with problems don't get the type of confrontation they need; they're not challenged as much as they need to be."

The problem of kids being "let off the hook" is dangerous, many experts say, because of the gateway principle of early drug use. According to this theory, the abuse of alcohol, marijuana, and tobacco in adolescence frequently leads to the later use of harder drugs like cocaine and heroin. Furthermore, the drug situation of the 1990s is much different than ever before. For one thing, drug abuse is starting at younger ages all the time. A 1989 Gallup poll revealed that the average age at which children first experiment with alcohol or marijuana is twelve. A separate study found that more than 700,000 children between the ages of twelve and seventeen had tried hallucinogens like LSD and PCP at least once. Secondly, drugs available to youngsters today are more potent than many substances of the past. The list of powerful drugs being used by adolescents today includes such well-knowns as crack, but others, like the hallucinogen Ecstasy, are appearing as well. Even marijuana, a popular "beginner's" drug, is much more potent now than it was in the 1970s. According to the National Institute on Drug Abuse, the level of THC (the active ingredient in marijuana) in a joint today is, on average, 5 to 15 times higher than it was twenty years ago.

THE WOODLANDS TREATMENT PROGRAM

Through a holistic approach to the problem of drug addiction, Woodlands promotes "recovery in all life areas." The components of the program are geared to meet the emotional, physical, educational, recreational, spiritual, and family needs of those in treatment. Throughout the program, the Twelve Steps of Alcoholics Anonymous (see table) are utilized, as are the support services of the local A.A. community. Some of the components of the Woodlands program include:

- daily therapy group
- daily school attendance (in-house)
- daily devotions
- daily Tenth Step group (taking personal inventory and admitting mistakes)
- A.A. attendance four to five times per week

- aerobic exercise four times per week
- YMCA four times per week
- educational topic groups three to four times per week
- group recreation twice a week.
- weekly individualized counseling
- weekly family visits
- weekly step study group. (Twelve Steps of A.A.)
- church attendance on Sunday (option to attend A.A. meeting on Sunday)
- bi-monthly sober parties
- quarterly trips

Director Andre-Krell explains the Woodlands treatment program as being "like a stool with three legs. We have to work on all three to achieve the right balance.

"The program is based on treating kids on three separate levels—cognitive, behavioral, and emotional," she says. "On the cognitive level, we make reading and writing assignments that make them think about themselves and how they've arrived at where they are in life. On the behavioral level, we have them doing things, activities that teach them how to interact and behave in healthy, responsible ways. Things like athletics or occupational therapy or visiting the library or doing some comparative shopping. And on the emotional level, the kids have to talk about their problems and discuss their feelings. That's a big part of their recovery. But all three areas need equal attention."

Like all residential rehabilitation facilities, Woodlands is not inexpensive. The approximate cost for treatment is $98 per day. Family contributions and state tax dollars cover about two-thirds of that cost; donations from some county governments with residents in treatment help to make up the shortfall. Typically, the Iowa Department of Human Services, the state agency covering part of the bill, asks to be reimbursed by the family based on its income level.

At every stage in the rehabilitation process, family contact is encouraged. The Woodlands handbook for residents and parents clearly states:

> *Since chemical dependency is a family illness and since one of Woodlands' goals is the reunification of the family, family involvement in treatment is crucial to recovery.*

Often, however, lack of family involvement impedes drug rehabilitation. "Nationally, the success rate for rehabilitation is low," says Julie Warden, "but most successes occur with higher family involvement. Some kids really suffer from uninvolved families." Visitation usually slumps badly around holidays, counselors say, because families tend to deny problems at such "festive" times.

Woodlands Treatment Center bears differences and shares similarities with other drug rehabilitation programs. One of the differences may be its emphasis on the role of spirituality in the recovery process. The Twelve Steps of Alcoholics Anonymous and the Christian foundations of Woodlands ensure that spirituality—but not necessarily religion—plays a big part in the client's recovery process.

"This is a Christian agency, so spirituality is probably more important here than it is in some other programs. But we don't push specific religious beliefs," explains Andre-Krell. "The residents don't even have to buy into Christianity if they don't want to. Some of them are more comfortable with using the Twelve Steps of A.A. as their higher power. We just encourage them to acknowledge the value of spirituality.

"As a recovering alcoholic, I can say that my sobriety depended on two things: learning how to have sober fun and my relationship with God. Spirituality is an important aspect of staying sober."

Like many other drug treatment programs, however, the Woodlands Treatment Center works toward rehabilitation in phases. Specifically, there are five phases to the program: Intake, Exploration, Action, Transition, and Real World. On average, it takes five months (not including the Real World phase) to complete the program. In order to graduate from Woodlands, residents must pass through each phase by satisfying the established requirements.

Intake

In the Intake Phase, the staff at Woodlands assesses the client's degree of drug dependency, social skills, educational level, and family functioning. At this time, the primary goal set for the client is to break through the denial of his substance abuse problems, according to Andre-Krell. This occurs through education about alcoholism and chemical dependency, honest discussions with the client and his family about drug use, compiling the list of 50 Insanities and 50 Interferences, and completion of the A.A. First Step (admitting one's powerlessness over addiction).

In addition, the client must work on two written assignments, one of which is an autobiography. The autobiography will help the young man review important times, events, and people in his life and possibly identify some past mistakes. The client must also complete a "Forces Paper," which is a short statement explaining why he is entering treatment.

The purpose of the Forces Paper is to have the client accept responsibility for his own circumstances, rather than assign the blame to another party. (Andre-Krell points out that the first draft of the Forces Paper usually contains an explanation such as "I'm at Woodlands because the judge sent me here." That excuse, however, is not acceptable. The paper must be revised until the client acknowledges his own responsibility.)

Within the first few weeks, the Woodlands staff assigns a primary counselor to each client and establishes a comprehensive treatment plan based on the unique problems he faces. Written assignments, in which clients address topics like anger, honesty, and self-centeredness, are given during this period. In addition, there are mandatory group sessions and other activities designed to help clients adjust to the therapeutic community.

Exploration

In the Exploration Phase, Andre-Krell explains, clients are "dredging up reasons for their drug use." The assignments and discussions during this period are intended to help residents focus on themselves and the personality characteristics that have led them to their current situations.

Goals of this phase include fully admitting chemical dependency (A.A. First Step), learning about oneself, identifying alternatives to drug use, and beginning to reestablish healthy family relationships. A.A. Steps Two to Five are to be completed in this period, and residents are expected to begin taking on added responsibilities, such as leading devotions. The autobiography begun in the Intake Phase must be completed before leaving the Exploration Phase.

During the Exploration Phase, residents may

also request home passes. The first such pass is generally for a four-hour period; gradual increases in time (up to twelve hours) may be permitted.

Action Phase

The Action Phase of the Woodlands treatment plan calls for residents to put into practice the principles they learned and explored in the first two phases of recovery. For example, clients must adopt recreational and social alternatives to drug use, attempt to overcome the character defects that led to their drug use, and cement their family relationships. This phase of the clients' treatment is the first step "toward weaning them back to normal living," says Andre-Krell.

At this point in their rehabilitation, residents at Woodlands are expected to complete A.A. Steps Six through Ten, attend four A.A. meetings per week, and find a sponsor within that group. (Sponsors are recovering alcoholics/addicts familiar enough with the A.A. recovery program to help a newcomer through the Twelve Steps.) In this period of treatment, clients may request home passes for twenty-four to thirty hours, and they are expected to attend A.A. meetings in their home town. In addition, since they are halfway through the rehabilitation program, residents in the Action Phase are expected to set examples for and assist new clients entering the program.

Transition Phase

In this next to last phase of the Woodlands program, clients make the transition back to their home community. With forty-eight-hour (or longer) passes, clients transfer into their home school district, obtain a graduate equivalency degree, or find a job. They also become active members of a local A.A.

group and set up a plan for their continued recovery (outpatient aftercare). They continue to have obligations at the Woodlands facility, such as leading devotions, participating in resident committees, and consultation with their primary therapist. The Eleventh and Twelfth Steps of A.A., which are spiritual steps and require the client's ongoing commitment, are also approached in this phase of rehabilitation.

Real World Phase

For those clients who stick with the program, the final phase of rehabilitation consists of moving back home with parents or into an independent living arrangement. The principles and attitudes that were taught by the Woodlands staff should be implemented in the client's daily life and he should take responsibility for his continuing recovery by participating in an aftercare program. To be recognized as a graduate of the Woodlands program, the client must also attend two Family Days with his parents at the Woodlands facility and deliver a graduation speech to the other residents within one month of entering the Real World Phase.

Unfortunately, completing treatment and becoming a graduate is not a very common event for most drug addicts in rehabilitation programs. Nationwide, the rate of successful completion is only about 50 percent. In four years, just seventeen adolescents at Woodlands have remained with the program through graduation, according to Andre-Krell. The others are usually discharged for one of two reasons: 1) Maximum Benefits, which means the individual has achieved all that he is capable of achieving in the program, but has not fulfilled the requirements for graduation; or 2) Non-compliance, which means the individual has exhibited exaggerated misbehavior, repeated violence, or other behavior that makes his continued participation in the Woodlands program impossible.

The typical client at Woodlands has a thorny past. Most have extensive first-hand experience with the criminal justice system. Most do not live with both natural parents. They frequently have a family history of alcohol or drug abuse and they almost always hang around with friends who use drugs. In short, they have lacked solid role models for personal development and opportunities for achievement.

"We're getting tougher and tougher kids," Andre-Krell observes. "Kids with dysfunctional families, kids with a lot of different types of damage. So treatment times are increasing and success rates are not as high as we'd like."

Still, the commitment to attacking drug abuse and dependency at its roots remains strong. Despite the increasingly difficult odds, Woodlands continues to pursue rehabilitation based on spiritual principles and a holistic approach that takes into account the many diverse aspects of each client's life. Despite the odds, the regular appearance of new drugs, and increasingly difficult cases, Woodlands remains a beacon of hope for young men trapped in the cycle of substance abuse.

CHAPTER SIX
THE COCAINE EPIDEMIC: SEARCHING FOR SOLUTIONS VIA TREATMENT

In the spring of 1990, a study by the United States Senate Judiciary Committee revealed the kind of news that no one really wanted to hear. The Senate report stated that there were an estimated 2.2 million cocaine addicts in the United States—two and a half times more than previous government estimates. The figures mean that one out of every one hundred Americans has a serious problem with coke. As if to underline the gravity of the cocaine threat, the report went on to say that one of every five people arrested for *any* crime is a so-called "hard core" coke addict.

While the release of the Senate report was certainly noteworthy, the fact that widespread addiction to cocaine—particularly crack cocaine—is wreaking havoc in cities and towns throughout the United States is relatively old news. After all, studies in the past three years have consistently shown cocaine addiction to be on the rise and its availability to be stubbornly high despite stepped up interdiction efforts. Crack, the smokable, most powerful form of cocaine,

CHART 5

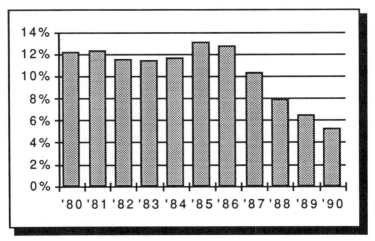

A national survey conducted by the University of Michigan's Institute for Social Research indicated that cocaine use among American high school students was in a downward trend. From a peak in 1985, when 13% of high school seniors reported using cocaine at least once in the previous year, use of the drug fell to 5.3% in 1990, according to the survey. The same study also showed that the use of crack cocaine among high school students had declined from 3.1% in 1989 to 1.9% in 1990. Since the study covered only enrolled high school students, there was no data on drug use patterns of dropouts, who are believed to be among the heaviest users of illegal drugs.

is all the more prevalent because its initial affordability makes it attractive to so many people. Most hard hit by the crack epidemic have been America's inner cities, where serious economic decay has resulted in widespread unemployment and social discontent. Selling drugs offers a rare opportunity to make some money, while using drugs offers an opportunity to temporarily escape a desperate situation.

Faced with crack's rapid spread across the country, many scientists and treatment specialists were baffled at first by what seemed to be the lightning-fast nature of the drug's addiction. Amazingly, many crack addicts reported being hooked after a single hit. For treatment centers used to treating individuals for alcohol, heroin, and other more "traditional" addictions, the arrival of crack cocaine was a menacing new invader.

"Two years ago, 90 percent of our clients were addicted to alcohol," says Irving Schandler, director of the Diagnostic and Rehab Center (DRC) in Philadelphia, Pennsylvania. "Today, 90 percent are addicted to crack cocaine. There's been a major shift here."

The dramatic shift toward crack as the new "drug of choice" occurred so quickly that many in the drug rehabilitation field were unprepared to deal with the challenge. Today, providers of drug treatment are still trying to come up with effective responses to the crack cocaine epidemic. Certain therapies seem to hold promise.

THE COCAINE ADDICTION

Before treatment approaches for the crack cocaine epidemic could be implemented, researchers needed to understand the drug's potent effect on the human body. Based on the experiences of users, it was known that cocaine produced a brief, but intense, euphoria (or high) followed quickly by severe depression (known as the crash). The empty feeling that inevitably followed the euphoria left many users wanting to regain their high. In this way, the cycle of cocaine use often became obsessive.

"I knew it [cocaine] was dangerous the first time I used it," says Bill M., a recovering addict seeking help through Narcotics Anonymous. He describes his experience with cocaine using words like "trapped."

"The high was better than anything else I'd ever tried," he says, "After that, all I could think about was getting high again. No matter what."

Researchers investigating the roller-coaster-like cycle of cocaine have discovered that the drug works by creating "over-excitement" in the brain. Introduced into the body by smoking, sniffing, or injection, cocaine quickly travels to the brain where it stimulates the release of *dopamine*, a naturally occurring chemical that makes human beings feel pleasure. However, unlike natural factors that stimulate the release of dopamine, cocaine also prevents the brain from reabsorbing the pleasure-producing chemical. This situation results in the extreme euphoria characteristic of a cocaine high. Eventually, the brain's supply of dopamine is exhausted, however, and the cocaine user experiences the crash.

By stimulating the brain, cocaine also excites other body systems, such as the digestive tract and the heart. Since crack is such a potent form of cocaine, its effects on the body are even more pronounced—and potentially lethal. Consider, for example, the muscles of the heart: Responding to crack, the brain sends messages to the heart that speed up its pumping action; if overstimulated, the heart can begin to beat erratically or stop beating completely. A testimony to the often fatal consequences of crack can be found in the much publicized death of University of Maryland basketball star Len Bias, who was using the drug shortly before he died.

Acknowledging the extreme effects of crack cocaine, many experts initially speculated that this form of addiction was virtually incurable. Crack cocaine addicts seemed to verify this opinion by their

CHART 6

Cocaine Deaths in Los Angeles County	
Year	No.
1974	1
1975	7
1980	32
1981	35
1982	74
1983	121
1984	377
1985	279
1986	736
1987	818
1988	1160

CHART 7

Modes of Death		
	No.	%
Nonviolent deaths		
overdose	32	72.7
illness	9	20.5
stillbirth	3	6.8
Violent deaths		
shot	30	42.4
stabbed	18	25.7
fell/jumped	6	8.6
auto accident	5	7.1
head trauma	4	5.7
strangled	2	2.9
drowned	2	2.9
auto vs. pedestrian	2	2.9
fire	1	1.4

A study of 114 Los Angeles County Coroner's cases in which cocaine was present found that more than 60% of the victims died a violent death. The researcher concluded: "Violence seems to be clearly connected to the use and abuse of cocaine." (Budd, R. D.: *American Journal of Drug and Alcohol Abuse,* 14:375–382, 1989.)

apparent willingness to seek out and use the drug, even at great personal risk or expense. As evidence, the National Institute on Drug Abuse has reported an alarming rise in the number of cocaine-related emergencies in hospitals. It is not uncommon, the report states, to find hospital emergency rooms, particularly in urban areas, literally overrun with individuals suffering or dying from cocaine intoxication.

Recently, however, some glimmer of hope has emerged for crack cocaine addicts. Although the epidemic itself shows no sign of relenting, treatment specialists say certain approaches to rehabilitation may offer crack addicts the opportunity to break the deadly cycle of drug use.

PROMISING SIGNS

The most difficult problem of crack cocaine addiction is the intense craving for the drug. Usually, this craving overrides all other considerations, including any concerns about personal health or the amount of money spent to support a crack habit. Acquiring more crack is all that matters. This being the case, most crack addicts never really consider the possibility of rehabilitation.

(Unfortunately, even for the relatively few crack addicts who come to the realization that they need help to regain control of their lives, opportunities for rehabilitation are scarce, especially in large cities. Most programs are overburdened. Caseloads at Philadelphia's DRC, for instance, have been cut from thirty per counselor to twenty in an effort to increase overall effectiveness. The move has increased the success rate for DRC's fourteen counselors, according to director Irving Schandler, but the reduction in caseloads means fewer slots are available to addicts in need of treatment.)

For those trying to rehabilitate crack addicts, the challenge is to attract users to treatment centers and keep them in the program long enough to break the pattern of drug use. Usually the opportunity comes after the addict has "hit bottom." In some cases, an addict who crashes after a severe bout of crack use will lie in a semicomatose condition for a full day or more. Upon awakening, it is possible that the addict may realize the seriousness of the situation and seek some help.

"For some people, there's a time when they hurt enough to show some interest in rehabilitation," says Irving Schandler. "That's when we want to get them into detoxification."

Most effective crack detoxification programs employ medicines that reduce the craving for cocaine and/or prevent the severe depression that follows its use. In the first weeks of treatment, when crack addicts are most likely to relapse and return to drug use, antidepressant medication can be the key to continued participation in a rehabilitation program. These medications offset the deep depression and anxiety that accompanies the cocaine crash, and may prove to be the bridge that allows crack addicts to pass from hopeless dependency to the first stages of rehabilitation.

Although still experimental, the urgency of the crack epidemic has prompted rehabilitation programs to implement the use of these medications. The initial results appear promising. One study found that the use of an antidepressant medication during the first three or four weeks of rehabilitation can double the number of crack addicts who stick with the program.

Another important aspect of the successful rehabilitation of crack addicts is an intensive, personalized counseling program that restores the recovering individual's self-esteem and holds out the hope of an eventual improvement in living conditions. This type of program often includes vocational or educational training designed to assist the addict in building a better life after treatment. Due to the nature of the cocaine addiction, this stage of rehabilitation frequently lasts about six months and most experts believe even this length of treatment will be useless unless the addict is in a controlled environment (that is, an inpatient setting).

"The one thing we've learned about treating crack cocaine addiction is that you've got to have a controlled environment plus intensive treatment," explains Schandler. "Particularly with crack cocaine, it's somewhere from difficult to impossible for people to control the addiction on an outpatient basis. The power of this drug is so great, and it is so addictive, that it's tremendously difficult to deal with it in an outpatient environment."

In addition to the overwhelming strength of the crack addiction itself, another difficulty facing those receiving treatment on an outpatient basis is that they usually remain in a setting that fosters continued drug use. At DRC in Philadelphia and in most other urban areas, crack addicts come from the inner city where crack use is rampant. Most are illiterate, and they usually have no family and no job to turn to for support. To return to that environment each day after receiving treatment would be self-defeating.

Long-term abstinence from crack cocaine is perhaps the most difficult task to accomplish. Even after six months of inpatient treatment, a recovering addict who returns to the same inner city streets from which he or she came is at high risk of relapse. The addict's friends probably still use crack and other drugs and, more often than not, the lack of decent jobs in the area makes drug trafficking one of the few viable money-making ventures. Certain strategies for avoiding common pitfalls can be taught in a rehabilitation program, but their effectiveness is of limited value in the face of a daily barrage of frustration and temptation.

Support groups like Narcotics Anonymous and Cocaine Anonymous or groups of individuals who have completed a specific treatment program (alumni organizations) are important buttresses against relapse. These kinds of aftercare services not only reinforce individuals by bringing them together with other recovering addicts, they are also outlets for drug-free socializing and relaxation. The principles of Cocaine Anonymous are an integral part of the rehabilitation effort at DRC, and continued participation in aftercare services is strongly encouraged.

Treatment experts agree, however, that no amount of rehabilitation or aftercare will do as much for long-term abstinence as will steady employment. With a job can come a sense of achievement that is so often lacking in the lives of crack addicts, as well as the means to support a drug-free life style. Of course, the prospects of landing a good job are not particularly encouraging for many recovering crack addicts. Not only do they usually lack the educational skills to compete for good jobs, but opportunities for decent employment are increasingly rare in the inner cities where many of them live. Vocational training and remedial education as part of drug rehabilitation programs can begin to address the problem of job training, but the scarcity of urban employers is a much broader dilemma.

In sum, the epidemic of crack cocaine addiction is perhaps the toughest illegal drug problem in the United States today. In terms of the number of people affected, the difficulties involved in rehabilitation, and the prospects for long-term abstinence, crack cocaine represents a serious affliction for American cities. To be sure, scientific investigation has shed new light on the bodily effects of cocaine. In turn, rehabilitation efforts have begun to respond to a challenge once thought insurmountable. But even though these new techniques have yielded some encouraging results, the odds remain desperate for many, if not most, inner city crack addicts. This is one problem that has roots deep in a societal crisis.

"I'd say we'll be fighting a losing battle for the next eight or nine years at least," predicts Schandler. "You have to realize that people get involved in drugs for many different reasons—running to or from one thing or another. In the ghetto, it's due to problems of housing, education, jobs, et cetera. These are the underlying problems and they simply are not being addressed."

CHAPTER SEVEN

AFTERCARE, TWELVE STEPS PROGRAM, AND RECOVERY THROUGH NARCOTICS ANONYMOUS

It's 8:00 P.M. on a Friday night in this midwestern college town. It's springtime, although the frosty 25-degree temperature indicates winter hasn't quite passed. People are on the move, going downtown to eat a pizza, catch a movie, or maybe have a few drinks with friends. Others head into the recreation facility to play racquetball or shoot some basketballs. It's a typical Friday night. The weekend is here and, while finals loom, there's still plenty of time to prepare. All in all, it's a good time to relax.

But upstairs in an old house across the street from the college's recreation building, there's a group of individuals feeling far from relaxed. About fifteen men and women—students and older adults—sit on folding chairs around a long cafeteria-style table. Cigarette smoke hangs thick in the small, crowded room as the discussion winds around the table, touching on people's frustrations, fears, and anxieties. This is the Friday night meeting of Narcotics Anonymous (N.A.).

I'm Jim and I'm an addict [a young man starts out]. I've had a pretty stressful week of classes. For one thing, there's this girl in my English class who's just really on my nerves. I don't know, it's not like she does anything, she just ticks me off, I guess. She's always got the assignments done, she always turns things in, she never screws up. She's always real happy, or at least acts like she's happy, and she comes up to me and pats me on the back like she knows me or something. I just can't handle it.

I'm trying to deal with my feelings about her. Honesty and all that, you know? Should I just tell her to shut up, or what? I don't really think that's the answer, but I'm getting real tired of her, I can tell you that. I know a lot of my attitude is from quitting [drugs] and everything and I'm really trying to cope. But I'm on edge . . .

This evening's gathering is just one of more than 16,000 such N.A. groups that meet in forty-three countries around the world. N.A. is a nonprofit organization of recovering drug addicts who meet regularly to share their feelings about the problems of drug addiction and the challenge of staying clean.

Not strictly a drug rehabilitation program, it would be more accurate to describe N.A. as a recovery program—a self-help organization of people trying to overcome their addictions. However, many people do use the N.A. program to rehabilitate themselves, while others come to N.A. for aftercare support following the completion of a professional drug rehabilitation program.

"The N.A. program is not really a treatment program per se," says Carl, a counselor at the N.A. World

102

Services Office in Van Nuys, California. (As its name implies, N.A. is an anonymous society, which means N.A. members are not identified by name outside of the organization.)

"There are no professionals or counselors, no authorities, and no fees. We approach the problem of addiction differently than most rehab centers. They have doctors, therapists, professional counselors. We're not doctors and we don't give medical advice. We just have experiences from our own lives to share with each other. We're also different in that our meetings are always open to anyone. Consider the waiting list at most treatment facilities."

Nationwide, the importance of all types of self-help groups—either as independent recovery programs or as supportive aftercare—is growing dramatically as drug treatment professionals attempt to address the difficult problems of relapse and incomplete recovery. Self-help groups like N.A. are among the few approaches that have demonstrated success in these areas. Since the recovery process can take months, years, or even an entire lifetime for some people, the need for an active, long-term support system is obvious. At times of severe uncertainty and anxiety, or even relatively minor stress, a support group can be the safety net that catches a faltering individual and prevents him or her from returning to active addiction. On a more routine basis, a support group can be the mechanism that makes drug- or alcohol-free living less of a strain by providing social outlets and opportunities for "sober fun."

Each particular N.A. group is self-supporting and autonomous, "except in matters affecting other groups or N.A. as a whole," according to the organization's guidelines. This means that meetings and other functions run according to the wishes of the individual members of the group.

CHART 8

The Twelve Steps of Narcotics Anonymous
1. We admitted that we are powerless over our addiction, that our lives had become unmanageable.
2. We came to believe that a Power greater than ourselves could restore us to sanity.
3. We made a decision to turn our will and our lives over to the care of God as we understood Him.
4. We made a searching and fearless moral inventory of ourselves.
5. We admitted to God, to ourselves, and to another human being the exact nature of our wrongs.
6. We were entirely ready to have God remove all these defects of character.
7. We humbly asked Him to remove our shortcomings.
8. We made a list of all persons we had harmed, and became willing to make amends to them all.

9. We made direct amends to such people whenever possible, except when to do so would injure them or others.

10. We continued to take personal inventory and when we were wrong promptly admitted it.

11. We sought through prayer and meditation to improve our conscious contact with God as we understood Him, praying only for knowledge of His will for us, and the power to carry that out.

12. Having had a spiritual awakening as a result of these steps, we tried to carry this message to addicts, and to practice these principles in all our affairs.

Most N.A. meetings open with a short statement by the group's chairperson. The statement may be a prayer or a reading from N.A.-sponsored literature, such as the organization's Preamble, which describes N.A.'s purpose. Sometimes other group members are asked to do a reading as well. Then, depending on the type of meeting taking place, a number of things can occur. If the meeting has been designated a "Closed Meeting" (for admitted addicts or those who think they have a drug problem), there is usually an informal discussion of problems or concerns, focusing on specific situations brought up by individuals in the group. Everyone in attendance has the opportunity to talk about anything they are feeling: happiness over a drug-free "anniversary," anger about a loved one's handling of a certain situation, fear of relapsing into drug use, and so on. Sometimes closed meetings focus on a specific topic, such as one of the Twelve Steps or a discussion of a passage from N.A. literature. Closed meetings are meant to strengthen the members and foster "group life" through an intimate exchange of thoughts.

Another common meeting format is the "Open Speaker Meeting" at which several N.A. members volunteer to speak to addicts and nonaddicts about their experiences with drugs. Usually the speakers talk about what their lives were like before they began recovery and how their circumstances have changed since they stopped using drugs. "Public Meetings" are similar gatherings, but the primary emphasis is on educating nonaddicts about N.A. Special members of the community, such as clergy, health care workers, and elected officials, may be invited to hear a guest speaker and learn about N.A. groups in the area. The goal of these open meetings is to develop ties to the nonaddict community and carry the N.A. message to new people. Most meetings are brought to an end by the group reciting a prayer, such as the Lord's Prayer or the Serenity Prayer (*God, grant me the serenity to accept the things I cannot change, the courage to change the things I can, and the wisdom to know the difference*).

THE TWELVE-STEPS APPROACH TO RECOVERY

N.A. is based on the principles established by Alcoholics Anonymous (A.A.), charging no fees and accepting anyone with a desire to stop using drugs. Since its founding in 1953, the mainstay of the organization has been the Twelve-Steps program, a system of recovery developed by A.A. and subsequently adapted for drug addicts (see table on page 104), and the group meeting, at which addicts freely discuss their feelings or problems.

Like its sister organization, N.A. emphasizes spiritual principles. Although not affiliated with any church or religious organizations, N.A. lists belief in "a Power greater than ourselves" among its Twelve Steps to recovery and encourages members to develop a relationship with their god, according to their own beliefs. The spiritual emphasis is apparent in other ways, as well. For example, it is interesting to note that nine of the Twelve Steps relate to internal actions or changes that the addict takes, while only three describe actions involving other people. This balance obviously points out the fact that N.A. concentrates on the transformation of the inner person. However, despite the importance placed on caring for oneself, persons involved in N.A. say that the ultimate outcome of practicing the Twelve Steps is an outward turn, a new connectedness with other people and a concern for family, friends, and other addicts. This paradox, they say, is what makes the Twelve Steps approach a success.

Members point out that the Twelve Steps are not commandments, rather they are "reports of action." In other words, the Twelve Steps describe the actions that practicing N.A. members have already taken in their progress toward recovery. They are a testimony from recovering addicts of the steps they followed to stop using drugs. New members who come to the meetings may not be able to recite all twelve steps, but it is hoped that gradually they will see the steps as actions they must take in order to begin or continue their recovery.

The absence of commandments and strict rules also influences the atmosphere of the N.A. program and the relationships that develop between practicing members. Those in the program say they are careful never to pressure fellow members into certain modes of behavior. While the program advocates complete abstinence from all drugs (including alcohol and marijuana), it does not set time schedules for abstinence, require attendance at meetings, or make other demands on members.

"We've never been open to being told, 'This is what you should be doing.' We've rebelled against that way of thinking. And as an addict, I understand that," Carl explains. "We're like a family where you're free to come and go. On a personal level, if one of our members was doing something dangerous, we might suggest that they seek some professional advice. But in general it's completely self-help, absolutely voluntary, and there's no strings attached."

The principle of anonymity also is established in this spirit of total acceptance. The purpose of the policy is to focus energy on the problems of drug addiction and the route to recovery rather than on personalities in the group. As stated in the N.A. Traditions, which describe the group's basic principles, "Anonymity is the spiritual foundation of all our

Traditions, ever reminding us to place principles before personalities." In addition, anonymity is important to many members who do not want their drug addictions to be known outside the group.

Like formal drug treatment programs, N.A. fosters open discussion of members' feelings, no matter what they may be: feelings of temptation to continue using drugs, uncertainty about the ability to quit using, resentment toward other individuals, and so on. The aim of such open discussion is to bring members face-to-face with a whole range of feelings, some of which have been suppressed or simply never experienced due to drug addiction. It is hoped that by confronting these emotions in the company of supportive, like-minded people, members can come to realize that their *response* to such feelings (not the feelings themselves) determines the long-term success of their recovery. The concept of honesty is central to these discussions. Members are encouraged to deal honestly with all their emotions by talking to others about how they feel rather than resorting to drug use to cover up their feelings.

Problems encountered in daily life also are on the table at an N.A. meeting. Often, such problems are not necessarily unique to addicts; many concerns are those facing everyone, addicts and nonaddicts alike: conflicts with a teacher, boss, spouse, child, boyfriend, or girlfriend; trouble with money and paying bills; the pressure to complete school or work projects on time; problems with confidence and self-esteem. The trouble is that drug use becomes an escape tactic through which addicts are able to avoid learning painful, but necessary, coping skills. Rather than confronting and dealing with the problems associated with everyday living, drug use provides a temporary, illusory diversion. Furthermore, drug addiction makes even relatively common problems more pressing and reduces the individual's ability to meet routine challenges.

> I'm Dave and I'm an addict. This is my first N.A. meeting and I've been off drugs for seven weeks. Right now I'm trying to deal with some feelings I haven't really had before. When I first decided to quit, I went out and got a haircut and bought some new clothes. Tried to change my image, you know. Well, some women I know and people I work with all told me how good I looked. I liked that a lot. It made me feel good that people noticed the change I made.
>
> But now, I'm not getting positive comments anymore. I guess people just take for granted that I show up for work on time and look decent rather than how I was when I was using drugs. I'm still thinking, 'God, this is a major change you've made,' but nobody else sees it that way anymore. It's like this is how I'm supposed to be so it's no big deal.
>
> I guess that's something I'm dealing with. Expectations.

The solution to such situations is not always easy, and the N.A. fellowship does not try to minimize people's problems. By encouraging the recovering addict to discuss frustrations and dilemmas and confront problems head on, soberly, with the support of friends and a higher power, N.A. promotes the idea that drug abuse is a false escape from real-world problems.

As might be expected of a program that focuses

on dealing honestly with oneself and one's feelings, N.A. recognizes the need to help its members achieve some very basic goals: resisting drug use one day at a time while developing values that will allow them to build and sustain meaningful relationships.

"Our program is based on the recovery process and understanding principles like honesty, commitment, and courage," Carl explains. "It sounds real simple, but it's not so easy for an addict. We're talking about people who are rebuilding their lives from the ground up, starting over from the very beginning. Establishing these types of values and principles is more difficult than it sounds."

N.A. SPONSORSHIP

Essentially, N.A. is based on the idea that individuals with drug problems are best qualified to help others like themselves. As one N.A. publication puts it, "There is a mutual respect and caring among clean addicts because we've all had to overcome the misery of addiction. We love and support each other in our recovery." The group meetings and the Twelve Steps continually reinforce this concept while helping members to rebuild normal lives.

One of the most important components in the process of rebuilding involves sponsorship, in which a member of the N.A. fellowship takes on the responsibility of assisting a newcomer in his or her recovery. At some point, most addicts in the N.A. program will work with a sponsor.

A sponsor is a recovering addict in the N.A. program who has progressed sufficiently toward recovery and can offer support and guidance to another recovering addict. Length of time in the N.A. program is not necessarily important—some members are in N.A. only a few months before becoming a sponsor—but sponsors need to have a thorough understanding of the Twelve Steps, feel comfortable with their own recovery, and be willing to help another addict.

"In a way, sponsorship is really the basis of the entire N.A. program—it's one addict helping another addict," says one N.A. member who has sponsored three newcomers. "But it's not like the sponsor is doing all the helping and the addict is getting all the help. It's a two-way street. The sponsor is still in the process of recovery, too, so the relationship helps him also. It means accepting a lot of responsibility and that is an important part of recovery."

Throughout the long recovery process, even after completing a formal rehabilitation program, it is common for an addict to experience severe anxiety and perhaps drift back toward drug use. At these times, sponsors can provide personal guidance and support. Drawing on their own experiences with drug addiction, sponsors can usually sympathize with the addict and offer much needed encouragement or advice. Sponsors, however, are not expected to be formal counselors. Their function is simply to help the recovering addict stay off drugs by sharing experiences and observations. Usually, there is daily contact between sponsor and addict, and both good and bad moments are discussed in a casual way. The resulting relationship that develops between the sponsor and addict is typically quite strong.

"I've opened up to my sponsor more than I've ever opened up to my wife," says one recovering addict. "There were things that I said to him that I thought would drive him away, but nothing ever did. He kept loving me and kept supporting me."

In another way, too, the sponsor-addict relationship can be beneficial. Many addicts assert that they've always been strong individualists, people who tend not to rely on others for much of anything. Substance abuse combined with this sense of individualism often leads to isolationism and distrust of others. Sponsorship, along with the spiritual principles that stress acceptance of a higher power, works against such isolationist tendencies and helps recovering addicts develop solid, trusting relationships with other people.

A RECOVERY PROGRAM THAT WORKS

To many outsiders, the Twelve Steps philosophy, which stresses recovery one day at a time, honesty with oneself and others, and a belief in a higher power, seems overly simplistic. Others criticize the program for relying on guilt tactics that they say are emotionally unfair. Perhaps the most stinging accusation made against Twelve Steps programs is that in trying to foster a safe, secure environment where troubled people can turn for support, these organizations enforce a type of conformity that prohibits individual expression or criticism of the group. But thousands of recovering drug addicts appear to be a testament to the effectiveness of N.A. Based on members alone, the system these addicts use to beat drug use must be given credit.

"The N.A. approach is based on spiritual principles—not religion. It's the idea that there's something more powerful, something beyond us that can help us recover," explains Carl. "When we do drugs, we are trying to control our lives. Maybe there have been problems that we felt were impossible to solve, so we turned to drugs as a way to control the situation.

"But obviously drug use hasn't worked either, and that realization can lead some people to despair. That's why it's critical to trust that you can get better. The N.A. program encourages addicts to trust other people and God. And when they do that they can get better. It works."

GLOSSARY

acquired immune deficiency syndrome (AIDS) - A
fatal virus that destroys the human immune system. The virus, transmitted through contact with
infected bodily fluids, such as blood, is spreading rapidly among many high-risk groups, including intravenous drug users who share
needles and syringes.

aftercare - Any of a variety of programs designed to
provide follow-up care to individuals who have
completed a drug-rehabilitation program. Services can include job training, counseling, and
opportunities for drug-free social interaction.

cannabis - The dried portions (usually the tops) of
hemp plants that are typically prepared into
marijuana or hashish and smoked.

codependency - An emotional and behavioral state
characterized by exaggerated concern for other
people or events and insufficient concern for
oneself. Codependency is theorized to arise from
any number of "dysfunctional" situations, in-

cluding the extremely stressful circumstances created by family members who are dependent on alcohol or drugs. Codependent individuals, who typically lack self-esteem and experience profound depression, may require treatment.

detoxification - The removal of toxic substances (e.g., drugs, alcohol, etc.) from the body. This can be achieved either through a regimen of prescribed medications or simply rest and proper nutrition.

dissociative anesthetics - Highly potent substances capable of producing intense and long-term psychic effects, including the sensation of complete separation from reality (e.g., angel dust, or PCP).

Drug Czar - The director of the Office of National Drug Control Policy. This office, created by Congress in 1988, is charged with coordinating the federal government's anti-drug initiatives. William Bennett was the first individual to hold this office.

halfway programs - Programs designed to ease the transition from inpatient treatment to independent living by providing an intermediate level of care. Such programs typically provide some supervision and counseling for a limited period of time before the client returns to his or her normal living situation.

hallucinogens - Substances that temporarily alter consciousness, affecting the way the user perceives his or her surroundings (e.g., marijuana, LSD, etc.). Also known as psychedelics.

inpatient treatment - Method of drug rehabilitation in which clients are removed from their normal surroundings and enter a hospital or specialized facility where they undergo treatment. Also known as **residential treatment.**

interdiction - Law-enforcement efforts to interrupt the supply of illegal drugs. Typical efforts include infiltration of suspected drug-smuggling operations, police seizure of illegal drugs, and crop-eradication programs in areas where illegal drugs are grown.

methadone - A man-made, long-acting narcotic that is used by some drug-rehabilitation facilities to break heroin addiction. While methadone satisfies the heroin addict's craving for opiates, it produces little or none of the euphoria associated with such drugs. Some methadone treatment programs strive for eventual abstinence while others are geared toward long-term maintenance.

narcotics - Drugs used to relieve pain and induce sleep (morphine, heroin, etc.). Usually addictive.

opiates - Drugs derived from opium (e.g., morphine, heroin, etc.).

outpatient treatment - Method of drug rehabilitation in which clients regularly visit a treatment center for guidance and counseling, but continue to live at home.

psychedelics - See **hallucinogens**.

psychoactive drugs - Substances that temporarily alter the body's central nervous system (e.g., uppers, downers, etc.).

resocialization - The process by which an individual is taught to reenter society and resume a productive life-style following completion of a drug-rehabilitation program.

sedative - A chemical agent that reduces the activity of body systems, including the central nervous system, the respiratory system, and the cardiac system (e.g., alcohol, barbiturates, etc.).

stimulant - A chemical agent that increases the activity of body systems, including the central nervous system, the respiratory system, and the

cardiac system (e.g., amphetamines, methamphetamines, etc., known as "speed").

Twelve Steps - A self-help plan designed to overcome addiction. The plan is based on open admission of one's powerlessness over substances
such as alcohol or drugs or particular behavior
patterns, support from others in similar situations, and the acceptance of a "Higher Power."

APPENDIX
DIRECTORY OF SELECTED DRUG REHABILITATION PROGRAMS IN THE UNITED STATES

NATIONAL INFORMATION CENTERS

Alcoholics Anonymous
General Service Office
Box 459
Grand Central Station
New York, NY 10163

The American Council for
  Drug Education
204 Monroe Street
Rockville, MD 20850
301-294-0600

Cocaine Anonymous
Central Office
6125 Washington Boulevard
Suite 203
Los Angeles, CA 90232
213-839-1141

National Clearinghouse for
  Alcohol and Drug
  Information
P.O. Box 2345
Rockville, MD 20850
301-468-2600

Narcotics Anonymous
World Service Office
16155 Wyandotte Street
Van Nuys, CA 91406
818-780-3951

PROGRAMS IN INDIVIDUAL STATES

ALABAMA

Fellowship House, Inc.
1625 12th Avenue
Birmingham, AL 35203
205-933-2430

St. Anne's Home, Inc.
2772 Hanover Circle
Birmingham, AL 35205
205-933-6906

Crestwood Hospital
New Start Program
One Hospital Drive
Huntsville, AL 35801
205-882-2121

119

Drug Education Council, Inc.
954 Government Street
Mobile, AL 36604
205-433-5456

St. Margaret's Hospital
Teen Unit
301 Ripley Street
Montgomery, AL 36104
205-269-8742

ALASKA

Alaska Council on
Prevention of Alcoholism
and Drug Abuse
7521 Old Seward Highway
Anchorage, AK 99502
907-349-6602

Aleutian Pribilof Island
Association
1689 C Street
Anchorage, AK 99501
907-276-2700

Fairbanks Substance Abuse
Center
3098 Airport Way
Fairbanks, AL 99709
907-474-0004

National Council on
Alcoholism
Juneau Unit
211 4th Street
Juneau, AK 99801
907-463-3755

Norton Sound Health
Corporation
Northern Lights Recovery
Center
5th Avenue and Division
Street
Community Health Services
Building
Nome, AK 99762
907-443-3344

ARIZONA

Tri City Community
Behavioral Health Center
1454 S. Dobson Road
Desert Samaritan Hospital
Mesa, AZ 85282
602-835-3655

Arizona Drug Abuse
Program
4901 W. Indian School Road
Phoenix, AZ 85031
602-247-5633

Good Samaritan Medical
Center
Community Treatment
Program
1118 E. Missouri Avenue
Phoenix, AZ 85014
602-241-0652

Phoenix Indian Center
1337 N. First Street
Phoenix, AZ 85004
602-256-2000

CODAC Counseling Center
of Pima County, Inc.
2530 E. Broadway, Suite D
Tucson, AZ 85716
602-327-4505

Tucson Alcoholic Recovery
Home, Inc.
1809 E. 23rd Street
Tucson, AZ 85713
602-622-9038

Crossing House Residential
Treatment Program
1070 W. First Street
Yuma, AZ 85364
602-782-3843

ARKANSAS

South Arkansas Regional
Health Center

Alcohol/Drug Treatment
Program
715 N. College Avenue
El Dorado, AR 71730
501-862-7921

Harbor House, Inc.
615 N. 19th Street
Forth Smith, AR 72901
501-785-4083

Northeast Arkansas
Women's Recovery Center
419 W. Jefferson Street
Jonesboro, AR 72401
501-932-0228

Twenty Four Hour Center,
Inc.
Men's Rehabilitation Center
2021 Main Street
Little Rock, AR 72206
501-375-7585

Twenty Four Hour Center,
Inc.
Women's Rehabilitation
Center
3900 Affolter Lane
Route 5
Little Rock, AR 72212
501-868-5184

CALIFORNIA

Anaheim Drug Abuse
Services
1133 N. Homer Street
Anaheim, CA 92801
714-490-5258

Alta Vista Chemical
Dependency Recovery
Hospital
301 E. Roberts Lane
Bakersfield, CA 93308
805-393-3000

Berkeley Asian Youth
Center
1950 Carleton Street

Room D-6
Berkeley, CA 94704
415-849-4898

Compton Special Services
Center
404 N. Alameda Street
Compton, CA 90221
213-605-5693

Breakthrough Adolescent
Program
125 E. Baker Street
Suite 280 North
Costa Mesa, CA 92626
714-432-8886

Fresno County Health
Department
Substance Abuse Program
1221 Fulton Mall, 6th Floor
Fresno, CA 93775
209-445-3272

Hispanic Alcoholism
Services Center of Orange
County
9842 W. 13th Street
Garden Grove, CA 92644
714-531-4624

Long Beach Alcohol and
Drug Rehabilitation
Program
Central Clinic
1133 E. Rhea Street
Long Beach, CA 90806
213-591-3381

Bay Area Addiction
Research and Treatment,
Inc.
Hollywood Clinic
8512 W. Whitworth Avenue
Los Angeles, CA 90035

California Detox Programs,
Inc.
Southeast Methadone Clinic
4920 S. Avalon Boulevard
Los Angeles, CA 90011
213-235-5035

121

Kaiser Permanente Alcohol
and Drug Dependency
Program
4733 Sunset Boulevard,
Room G02
Los Angeles, CA 90027
213-667-8206

Mujeres Recovery Home for
Hispanic Women
530 N. Avenue 54
Los Angeles, CA 90024
213-254-3769

Stanislaus County
Substance Abuse Services
1501 F Street
Modesto, CA 95354
209-525-7460

Napa County Human
Services Alcoholism and
Drug Abuse Program
2344 Old Sonoma Road
Napa, CA 94558
707-253-4721

The 14th Street Clinic and
Medical Group
1124 E. 14th Street
Oakland, CA 94602
415-533-0800

American Indian Substance
Abuse Program, Inc.
Turquoise Indian Lodge
2727 P Street
Sacramento, CA 95816
916-456-3487

Scripps Clinic and Research
Foundation
Alcohol/Chemical
Dependency Program
15025 Innovation Drive
San Diego, CA 92128
619-487-1800, Ext. 1327

Haight Asbury Free Medical
Clinic
Drug Detoxification Youth
Project

529 Clayton Street
San Francisco, CA 94117
415-621-2015

Presidio Community
Counseling Center
Presidio of San Francisco
Building 910
San Francisco, CA 94129
415-561-3784, Ext. 5433

Santa Clara County Drug
Abuse Services
Downtown Medical Clinic
1075 E. Santa Clara Street
San Jose, CA 95116
408-288-9120

Cottage Care Center
2415 De La Vina Street
Santa Barbara, CA 93105
805-682-2511

COLORADO

Aurora Center for Treatment
15400 E. 14th Place, Suite
433
Aurora, CO 80011
303-344-9750

Boulder Alcohol
Educational Center
1300 Canyon Boulevard,
Room 2
Boulder, CO 80302
303-444-6142

El Paso County Health
Department
Alcohol/Drug Treatment
Program
710 S. Tejon Street
Colorado Springs, CO 80903
719-578-3150

Centre at Porter Hospital
Substance Abuse Program
2525 S. Downing Street
Denver, CO 80210
303-778-5774

Substance Treatment
  Services
645 Bannock Street
Denver, CO 80204
303-893-7830

Adult/Adolescent Alcohol
  Treatment
1001 Patterson Road
Grand Junction, CO 81501
303-245-6624

Pueblo Treatment Services,
  Inc.
1711 E. Evans Avenue
Pueblo, CO 81004
719-546-6666

CONNECTICUT

Regional Network of
  Treatment Programs
Golden Hill Treatment
  Center
171 Golden Hill Street
Bridgeport, CT 06604
203-333-4105

Danbury Youth Services,
  Inc.
32 Stevens Street
Danbury, CT 06810
203-748-2936

Community Health Services
Comprehensive Substance
  Abuse Program
520 Albany Avenue
Hartford, CT 06120
203-249-9625

Rushford Treatment Center
77 Crescent Street
Middletown, CT 06457
203-346-0300

APT Foundation, Inc.
904 Howard Avenue
New Haven, CT 06519
203-787-7188

Crossroads, Inc.
48 Howe Street
New Haven, CT 06511
203-865-3541

Central Naugatuck Valley
  Help, Inc.
900 Watertown Avenue
Waterbury, CT 06708
203-756-8984

Morris Foundation, Inc.
26 N. Elm Street
Waterbury, CT 06702
203-755-1143

DELAWARE

Recovery Center of
  Delaware
Governor Bacon Health
  Center
Delaware City, DE 19706
302-836-1593

Kent County Counseling
  Services
811 S. Governors Avenue
Dover, DE 19901
302-736-4548

Division of Alcoholism,
  Drug Abuse and Mental
  Health
1901 N. DuPont Highway
New Castle, DE 19720
302-421-6101

Brandywine Counseling and
  Diagnostic Center, Inc.
305 W. 12th Street
Wilmington, DE 19801
302-656-2348

Sodat Counseling and
  Evaluation Center
1606 W. 16th Street
Wilmington, DE 19806
302-656-4044

DISTRICT OF COLUMBIA

Alcohol and Drug Abuse
   Services Administration
Detoxification Center
1905 E Street, S.E.
Ugast Building
Washington, D.C. 20003
202-727-5163

Bureau of Rehabilitation,
   Inc.
Community Care Center
3301 16th Street
Washington, D.C. 20010
202-842-7048

Rehabilitation Services
   Administration
Alcohol and Drug Abuse
   Section
1300 First Street, N.E.
Suite 114
Washington, D.C. 20002
202-727-2628

Seton House at Providence
   Hospital
1053 Buchanan Street, N.E.
Washington, D.C. 20017
202-269-7777

The Substance Abuse
   Multi-Purpose Treatment
   and Training Center
1300 First Street, N.W.
Washington, D.C. 20002
202-727-5161

FLORIDA

Dependency Awareness and
   Treatment Center at
   Horizon Hospital
11300 Highway 19 South
Clearwater, FL 34624
813-541-2646, Ext. 232

Humana Hospital Daytona
   Beach
Alcohol and Drug Help Unit

400 N. Clyde Morris
   Boulevard
Daytona Beach, FL 32014
904-239-5084

Broward County Addiction
   Rehabilitation Center
1000 S.W. 2nd Avenue
Fort Lauderdale, FL 33312
305-765-5868

Southwest Florida
   Addiction Services, Inc.
2150 W. First Street, Suite
   2B
Fort Myers, FL 33901
813-337-4411

Gateway Community
   Services, Inc.
555 Stockton Street
Jacksonville, FL 32204
904-387-5603

Dade County Alcohol and
   Drug Abuse Program
Human Resources Health
   Center
2500 N.W. 22nd Avenue
Miami, FL 33142
305-638-6540

North Miami CMHC
Substance Abuse Treatment
   Program
9400 N.W. 12th Avenue
Miami, FL 33150
305-691-0091

Office of Rehabilitative
   Services
Central Methadone Clinic
1600 N.W. 3rd Avenue
Miami, FL 33126
305-579-2820

The Center for Drug Free
   Living
100 W. Columbia Street
Orlando, FL 32806
305-423-6606

Lakeview Center, Inc.
1221 W. Lakeview Avenue
Pensacola, FL 32501
904-432-1222

DACCO Central Intake
202 E. 7th Avenue
Tampa, FL 33602
813-273-9190

Hanley Hazelden Center at
 Saint Mary's
5200 E. Avenue
West Palm Beach, FL 33407
305-848-1666

GEORGIA

Northeast Georgia Alcohol
 and Drug Abuse
 Prevention and Treatment
1247 Prince Avenue
Athens, GA 30606
404-542-8656

DeKalb Substance Abuse
 Services
1260 Briarcliff Road, N.E.
Atlanta, GA 30306
404-894-5808

Northside Comprehensive
 CMHC
Alcohol and Drug Abuse
 Treatment Program
1000 Johnson Ferry Road,
 N.E.
Atlanta, GA 30342
404-851-8950

CMHC of East Central
 Georgia
Alcohol and Drug Services
3405 Old Savannah Road
Georgia Regional Hospital
Building 15
Augusta, GA 30906
404-790-2983

Chatham Clinic for
 Addictions

607 Abercorn Street
Savannah, GA 31401
912-651-2194

HAWAII

Anodyne Inc./DUI and
 Chemical Dependency
 Treatment Programs
1188 Bishop Street, Suite
 3204
Honolulu, HI 96813
808-545-7706

Hawaii Substance Abuse
 Information Center
200 N. Vineyard Boulevard
Suite 603
Honolulu, HI 96817
808-536-7234

Castle Memorial Hospital
Alcohol Addictions Program
640 Ulukakini Street
Kailua, HI 96734
808-263-4429

Alcoholic Rehabilitation
 Services of Hawaii, Inc.
45-710 Keaahala Road
Kaneohe, HI 96744
808-235-4531

Teen Challenge Maui
Olowalu Village
Wailuku, HI 96793
808-661-3914

IDAHO

Road to Recovery, Inc.
583 W. Sexton Street
Blackfoot, ID 83221
208-785-6688

Northwest Passages
 Adolescent Hospital
131 N. Allumbaugh Street
Boise, ID 83704
208-322-5922

The Nelson Institute
1010 N. Orchard Street
Suite 1
Boise, ID 83706
208-377-8204

Port of Hope North
202 Anton Street
Coeur D'Alene, ID 83814
208-664-3300

Port of Hope West
Payette Outpatient Office
208 N. 8th Street
Payette, ID 83661
208-642-2237

ILLINOIS

Hill House Outpatient
   Services
406 W. Mill Street
Carbondale, IL 62901
618-529-1151

Prairie Center for Substance
   Abuse
122 W. Hill Street
Champaign, IL 61820
217-359-1160

Brass Dual Diagnosis
514 E. 50th Place
Chicago, IL 60615
312-538-3400

Cuneo Hospital
Women's Chemical
   Dependence Program
750 W. Montrose Avenue
Chicago, IL
312-883-8200

Garfield Counseling Center
4010 W. Madison Street
Chicago, IL 60624
312-533-8500

Lutheran Social Services of
   Illinois
Alcohol/Drug Dependence
   Program

4840 W. Byron Street
Chicago, IL 60641
312-282-7800 Ext. 237

Substance Abuse Services,
   Inc.
2101 S. Indiana Avenue
Chicago, IL 60616
312-663-3610

Rock Island County Council
   on Addictions
Route 2
East Moline, IL 61244
309-792-0292

Comprehensive Mental
   Health Center of St. Clair
   County, Inc.
Alcoholism and Drug Abuse
   Services
3911 State Street
East St. Louis, IL 62205
618-482-7350

Lifeworks Chemical
   Dependency Center
214 N. Ottawa Street
Joliet, IL 60431
815-727-4611

Human Service Center
600 Fayette Street
Peoria, IL 61603
309-671-8000

Addiction Treatment and
   Education Program
2400 N. Rockton Avenue
Rockford, IL 61130
815-968-6861, Ext, 5201

Illinois Alcoholism and
   Drug Dependence
   Association
500 W. Monroe Street, 3rd
   Floor
Springfield, IL 62704
217-528-7335

INDIANA

South Central CMHC
Substance Abuse Services
645 S. Rogers Street
Bloomington, IN 47401
812-339-1619

South West Indiana Mental
  Health Center, Inc.
613 Cherry Street
Evansville, IN 47713
812-425-3305

Washington House, Inc.
2720 Culbertson Street
Fort Wayne, IN 46802
219-432-8684

Gary CMHC, Inc.
1100 W. 6th Avenue
Gary, IN 46402
219-885-4264, Ext. 300

Fairbanks Hospital
Indianapolis Counseling
  Center
Substance Abuse Program
8180 Clearvista Parkway
Indianapolis, IN 46256
317-842-4551

Prevention Intervention
  Treatment Services
2236 E. 10th Street
Indianapolis, IN 46201
317-633-8240

Dunn Mental Health Center
831 Dillon Drive
Richmond, IN 47375
317-983-8100

IOWA

Regional Substance Abuse
  Center, Inc.
713 S. Duff Street
Ames, IA 50010
515-232-3206

Young House Family
  Services, Inc.
Woodlands Treatment
  Center
RR 1, Box 217
Burlington, IA 52601
319-753-0700

Hillcrest Family Services
Chemical Dependency
  Program
1727 First Avenue, S.E.
Cedar Rapids, IA 52402
319-362-3149

Country Oaks
12160 S. Utah Avenue
Davenport, IA 52804
319-326-1150

Mercy Hospital Medical
  Center
Alcohol and Drug Recovery
  Program
6th and University
Des Moines, IA 50314
515-247-4441

Native American Treatment
  Program, Inc.
2720 Larpenteur Avenue
Sioux City, IA 51110
712-277-9416

MECCA-Substance Abuse
  Services
430 Southgate Ave.
Iowa City, IA 52240
319-351-4357

KANSAS

Mental Health Center of
  East Central Kansas
Alcohol and Drug Services
1305 W. 12th Street
Emporia, KS 66801
316-342-6116

127

Substance Abuse Center of
Eastern Kansas, Inc.
4125 Rainbow Boulevard
Kansas City, KS 66103
913-361-0045

Manhattan Medical Center
Alcohol and Drug Abuse
Services
1133 College Avenue
Building B, Upper Level
Manhattan, KS 66502
913-537-4014

Central Kansas Foundation
for Alcohol and Chemical
Dependency
903 E. Prescott Street
Salina, KS 67401
913-825-6224

Mid-American All Indian
Center
Indian Alcohol Treatment
Services
313 N. Seneca Street
Wichita, KS 67203

KENTUCKY

Pathways, Inc.
2162 Greenup Avenue
Ashland, KY 41101
606-324-1141

Bluegrass Education and
Treatment
Wash Road
Route 7
Frankfort, KY 40601
502-223-2017

Bluegrass East
Comprehensive Care
Center
201 Mechanic Street
Lexington, KY 40508
606-233-0444

St. Joseph Hospital
Center for Chemical
Independency
One St. Joseph Drive
Lexington, KY 40503
606-276-4597

Brooklawn Treatment
Center, Inc.
2125 Goldsmith Lane
Louisville, KY 40218
502-451-5177

LOUISIANA

Lafayette Alcohol and Drug
Abuse Clinic
400 St. Julien Street, Suite 1
Lafayette, LA 70506
318-265-5870

Bright House
Bright House for Women
201 Bright Street
Monroe, LA 71201
318-323-4243

Desire Narcotic
Rehabilitation Center, Inc.
3307 Desire Parkway
New Orleans, LA 70126
504-945-8885

New Orleans Adolescent
Hospital
Substance Abuse Unit
210 State Street
New Orleans, LA 70118
504-897-4691

Chemical Dependency
Services, Inc.
2124 Fairfield Avenue
Shreveport, LA 71104
318-227-2124

Manna Adolescent
Substance Abuse Center
4900 Mansfield Road
Shreveport, LA 71108
318-868-6552

MAINE

Crisis and Counseling
  Center
79 Sewall Street
Augusta, ME 04330
207-623-4511

Eastern Maine Medical
  Center
Chemical Dependency
  Institute
489 State Street
Bangor, ME 04401
207-945-7272

Aroostook Mental Health
  Center
Alcoholism and Drug
  Services
1 Vaughn Place
Caribou, ME 04736
207-498-6431

Tri County Mental Health
  Services
Substance Abuse
  Counseling Services
465 Main Street
Lewiston, ME 04240
207-783-4676

Evodia House DHRS, Inc.
48 Cedar Street
Portland, ME 04101
207-718-7458

MARYLAND

Annapolis Youth Service
  Bureau
92 W. Washington Street
Annapolis, MD 21401
301-224-1761, Ext. 1763

Baltimore Adolescent
  Treatment Program
4940 Eastern Avenue
B-3-S
Baltimore, MD 21224
301-955-0149

Baltimore Recovery Center
16 S. Poppleton Street
Baltimore, MD 21201
301-685-2811

Johns Hopkins Hospital
Program for Alcohol and
  Other Drug Dependencies
708 N. Broadway
Baltimore, MD 21205
301-955-5439

X-Cell, Inc.
Spring Grove State Hospital
Garrett Building
Baltimore, MD 21228
301-788-2145

Allegany County Addictions
  Program
Residential and Outpatient
Willowbrook Road
Cumberland, MD 21505
301-777-5680

Washington County Health
  Department
1302 Pennsylvania Avenue
Hagerstown, MD 21742
301-791-3042

Ethos Foundation
10701 Old Georgetown Road
Rockville, MD 20852
301-493-6447

MASSACHUSETTS

Boston Chinese Youth
Essential Services
199 Harrison Avenue
Boston, MA 02111
617-482-4243

Peaceful Movement
  Committee, Inc.
150 American Legion
  Highway
Boston, MA 02124
617-436-3159, Ext. 40

129

Bournewood Hospital
Substance Abuse Treatment
  Program
300 South Street
Brookline, MA 02146
617-739-1424

Concilio Addictions
  Program
105 Windsor Street
Cambridge, MA 02139
617-661-8000

Lifeline
Methadone Treatment
795 Middle Street
St. Anne's Hospital
Fall River, MA 02721
508-674-5741, Ext. 2260

Beacon House for Men
53 Beacon Street
Greenfield, MA 01301
413-773-8020

Beacon House for Women
153 High Street
Greenfield, MA 01301
413-774-5378

Center for Family
  Development of Greater
  Lowell, Inc.
45 Merrimack Street
Lowell, MA 01852
508-459-2306

Prevention One
76 Pleasant Street
Northampton, MA 01060
413-584-3880

Counseling Centers of
  Western Massachusetts
Springfield Site
150 Sumner Avenue
Springfield, MA 01108
413-732-2553

Bancroft Human Services,
  Inc.
25 Quinsigamond Avenue

Worcester, MA 01608
508-755-7118

Prospect House, Inc.
110 Lancaster Street
Worcester, MA
508-799-0702

MICHIGAN

Clear House Chemical
  Dependency Program
704 Spring Street
Ann Arbor, MI 48103
313-663-2500

New Addictions Treatment
Adolescent Service
165 N. Washington Avenue
Battle Creek, MI 49016
616-964-7121

Eleonore Hutzel Recovery
  Center
301 E. Hancock Street
  Detroit, MI 48201
313-745-7411

Family Services of Detroit
Central District Office
220 Bagley Street
Michigan Building, Suite
  224
Detroit, MI 48226
313-965-2141

Neighborhood Service
  Organization
24-Hour Walk-In Center
54 W. Henry Street
Detroit, MI 48201
313-963-1525

Treatment Alternatives to
  Street Crime
Main Drug Intake
1200 6th Street, Mezzanine
Detroit, MI 48226
313-256-2573

130

Koala Center
Day Treatment
1207 N. Ballenger Highway
Flint, MI 48504
313-767-1190

Community Services
Project Rehab
822 Cherry Street, S.E.
Grand Rapids, MI 49506
616-458-8521

New Horizons
Specialized Treatment for
  Cocaine Dependency
935 N. Washington Street
Suite 203
Lansing, MI 48906
517-482-0033

Southland Counseling
  Center
Substance Abuse Treatment
  Program
808 Southland Street
Lansing, MI 48910
517-393-0150

MINNESOTA

2001/Young People's
  Residential Treatment
  Center
2001 W. 3rd Street
Duluth, MN 55806
218-726-2201

Northland Mental Health
  Center
Substance Abuse Services
215 2nd Avenue, S.E.
Grand Rapids, MN 55744
218-326-1274

Addictions and Stress
  Clinics, Ltd.
201 N. Broad Street, Suite
  202
Mankato, MN 56001
507-345-4670

Eden Youth Program
1035 E. Franklin Avenue
Minneapolis, MN 55404
612-874-9441

Hazelden Foundation
15245 Pleasant Valley Road
Center City, MN 55025
612-257-4010

Hazelden Women's
  Outpatient Program
1400 Park Avenue
Minneapolis, MN 55404
612-348-9445

Minnesota Indian Women's
  Resource Center
1900 Chicago Avenue
Minneapolis, MN 55404
612-872-8211

Zumbro Valley Crisis
  Receiving Unit
2116 S.E. Campus Drive
Rochester, MN 55903
507-288-8750

Stepping Stones
Chemical Dependency
  Services, Inc.
4651 Nicols Road, Suite 200
St. Paul, MN 55122
612-454-6739

MISSISSIPPI

Jackson Mental Health
  Center
Alcohol and Drug Abuse
  Program
969 Lakeland Drive
St. Dominic Jackson
  Memorial Hospital
Jackson, MS 39216
601-364-6103

131

Mississippi Baptist Medical
  Center
Chemical Dependency
  Center
1225 N. State Street
Jackson, MS 39201
601-968-1106

Singing River Mental Health
  Center
Alcohol and Drug Program
4507 McArthur Street
Pascagoula, MS 39567
601-769-1793

Region III Chemical
  Dependency Program
Highway 78 East, Route 2
Tupelo, MS 38801
601-844-3531

Marian Hill Chemical
  Dependency Center
100 McAuley Drive
Vicksburg, MS 39180
601-631-2700

MISSOURI

Cape Girardeau Wiser, Inc.
233 Independence Street
Cape Girardeau, MO 63701
314-334-4303

Family Counseling Center of
  Missouri, Inc.
Alcohol/Drug Treatment
  Services
1001 E. Walnut Street, Suite
  202
Columbia, MO 65201
314-449-2581

Hannibal Council on
  Alcohol and Drug Abuse,
  Inc.
Main Unit
121 S. 10th Street
Hannibal, MO 63401
314-248-1196

Whispering Oaks Hospital
Adolescent Psychiatric
  Treatment Hospital
1314 W. Edgewood Drive
Jefferson City, MO 65101
314-634-5000

Greater Kansas City Mental
  Health Foundation
Outpatient/Inpatient
  Component
712 E. Linwood Boulevard
Kansas City, MO 64109
816-756-1391

Kansas City Community
  Center
1514 Campbell Street
Kansas City, MO 64108
816-421-6670

Renaissance West, Inc.
Administrative Unit
425 E. 63rd Street, Suite
  100–110
Kansas City, MO 64110
816-444-0733

DART, Inc.
1307 Lindbergh Plaza
  Center
St. Louis, MO 63132
314-569-3105

New Beginnings Program
2639 Miami Street
St. Louis, MO 63118
314-577-5849

Progressive Youth Center
2842 N. Ballas Road
St. Louis, MO 63131
314-569-1277

MONTANA

South Central Montana
  Mental Health Center
Alcohol and Drug Services

1245 N. 29th Street
Billings, MT 59101
406-252-5658

Providence Alcohol and
 Drug Center
401 3rd Avenue North
Great Falls, MT 59401
406-727-2512

Boyd Andrew Service
 Center
219 N. Rodney Street
Helena, MT 59601
406-443-2343

Recovery Foundation
554 W. Broadway
Missoula, MT 59802
406-721-1880

Montana State Hospital
Lighthouse Chemical
 Dependency Center
Galen Campus
Warm Springs, MT 59756
406-693-7351

NEBRASKA

Northwest Nebraska Alcohol
 and Drug Abuse Services
300 W. 2nd Street
Chadron, NE 69337
308-432-4416

North Central Alcoholism
Outpatient Counseling
 Services
2112 W. Faidley Street
Memorial Health Center
Grand Island, NE 68803
308-381-5622

Houses of Hope of
 Nebraska, Inc.
2501 South St.
Lincoln, NE 68502
402-435-5319

Region 2 Substance Abuse
 Services
110 N. Bailey Street
North Platte, NE 69101
308-543-6029

Immanuel Medical Center
Family Counseling Center
7836 Wakeley Plaza
Tower Professional Building
Omaha, NE 68154
402-399-8321

United Catholic Social
 Services
The Shelter
Omaha, NE 68104
402-558-5700

NEVADA

Community Addiction
 Clinic
625 Fairview Drive, Suite
 116
Carson City, NV 89701
702-882-3945

Vitality Center
3740 E. Idaho Street
Elko, NV 89801
702-738-8004

Nevada Treatment Center
1721 E. Charleston
 Boulevard
Las Vegas, NV 89104
702-382-4226

Western Counseling
 Associates Youth
 Programs
401 S. Highland Street
Las Vegas, NV 89106
702-385-3330

Northern Area Substance
 Abuse Council
320 Flint Street
Reno, NV 89501
702-786-6563

NEW HAMPSHIRE

Central New Hampshire
 Community Mental
 Health Services
 Administration
5 Market Lane
Concord, NH 03301
603-228-1551

Office of Youth Services
36 Lowell Street
Manchester, NH 03101
603-624-6470

Nashua Alcohol and Drug
 Counseling Services
18 Mulberry Street
Nashua, NH 03060
603-889-1090

Monadnock Region
Substance Abuse Services
 Inc.
Main Street P.O. Box 196
Keene, NH 03431
603-357-3007

Seacoast Mental Health
 Center
Administrative Unit
1145 Sagamont Avenue
Portsmouth, NH 03801
603-431-6703

Carrol County Mental
 Health
Substance Abuse Services
Huggins Hospital
Wolfeboro, NH 03894
603-569-1884

NEW JERSEY

Institute for Human
 Development
1315 Pacific Avenue
Atlantic City, NJ 08401
609-345-4035

Substance Abuse Center of
 Southern Jersey, Inc.

417 Broadway
Camden, NJ 08103
609-757-9190

East Orange Substance
 Abuse Program
160 Halsted Street
East Orange, NJ 07018
201-266-5200

Hunterdon Medical Center
Center for Alcohol and
 Substance Abuse
Route 31
Flemington, NJ 08822
201-788-6401

The Harbor
1405 Clinton Street
Hoboken, NJ 07030
201-656-4040

Damon House of New
 Brunswick
105 Joyce Kilmer Avenue
New Brunswick, NJ 08901
201-828-6002

Integrity, Inc.
103 Lincoln Park
Newark, NJ 07102
201-623-0600

The New Well Addict
 Rehabilitation Center
15 Roseville Avenue
Newark, NJ 07101
201-242-0715

Straight and Narrow, Inc.
396 Straight Street
Paterson, NJ 07501
201-345-6000

New Horizon Treatment
 Services, Inc.
132 Perry Street, 2nd Floor
Trenton, NJ 08618
609-394-8988

NEW MEXICO

La Placita Reintegration
  Center
Substance Abuse Program
3102 N. Florida Street
Route 7
Alamogordo, NM 88310
505-434-0515

Albuquerque Indian
  Hospital
Chemical Abuse Unit
801 Vassar Drive, N.E.
Community Health Building
Albuquerque, NM 87106
505-256-4000

South Broadway Youth
  Development Inc.
1500 Walter Street, S.E.
Albuquerque, NM 87102
505-854-2543

Southwest Counseling
  Center, Inc.
1480 N. Main Street
Las Cruces, NM 88001
505-526-3371, Ext. 112

Santa Fe Group Homes
La Nueva Vida
1301 Luisa Street
Santa Fe, NM 87501
505-983-9521

NEW YORK

Albany County Substance
  Abuse Clinic
59 S. Ferry Street
Albany, NY 12202
518-445-7888

St. Peter's Alcoholism
  Rehabilitation Center
315 S. Manning Boulevard
Albany, NY 12208
518-454-1356

Fairview Halfway House, Inc.
Fairview Information and
  Referral

38 Carroll Street
Binghamton, NY 13901
607-722-4080

Archdiocese Drug Abuse
  Prevention Program
1725 Castle Hill Avenue
Bronx, NY 10462
212-904-1333

Van Etten Hospital Drug
  Treatment Program
Methadone Maintenance
  Treatment Program
Morris Park and Seminole
  Avenues
Nathan Van Etten Hospital,
  Ward 1A
Bronx, NY 10461
212-829-3440

Dynamic Youth Community,
  Inc.
1830 Coney Island Avenue
Brooklyn, NY 11230
718-376-7923

Interfaith Medical Center
555 Prospect Place
Brooklyn, NY 11238
718-467-7000

City of Buffalo
Division of Substance Abuse
  Services
65 Niagara Square, 21st Floor
Buffalo, NY 14202
716-851-4014

Legal Aid Bureau of Buffalo,
  Inc.
656 Elmwood Avenue, Suite
  300
Buffalo, NY 14222
716-884-3256

Nassau County Medical
  Center Detoxification Unit
2201 Hempstead Turnpike,
  10 West
East Meadow, NY 11554
516-542-2394

135

Samaritan Village, Inc.
97–77 Queens Boulevard,
Suite 616
Flushing, NY 11374
718-897-4500

Warwick Area Migrant
Committee
Farm Workers Community
Center
Pulaski Highway
Road 2
Goshen, NY 10924
914-651-4272

Queens County Youth
Development Corp.
89–15 Woodhaven
Boulevard
Jamaica, NY 11421
718-847-9233

Ulster County Mental
Health Service
Methadone Maintenance
and Rehabilitation
Program
Golden Hill Drive
Kingston, NY 12401
914-331-6949, Ext. 253

Addicts Rehabilitation
Center Fund, Inc.
1881 Park Avenue
New York, NY 10035
212-427-1342

Children's Aid Society
Drug Intervention Program
105 E. 22nd Street
New York, NY 10010
212-949-4927

Daytop Village, Inc.
54 West 40th Street
New York, NY 10018
212-354-6000

Ecumenical Narcotic
Treatment for Effective
Rehabilitation
Residential and Outpatient
Units

252 E. 112th Street
New York, NY 10029
212-860-2460

Greenwich House
Counseling Center
80 5th Avenue, 10th Floor
New York, NY 10011
212-691-2900

Kaleidoscope
13206 W. 125th Street
New York, NY 10027
212-678-1277

Lower East Side Service
Center
Methadone Treatment
Program
62 E. Broadway
New York, NY 10003
212-431-4610

New York State Division of
Substance Abuse Services
80 Centre Street, No. 332
New York, NY 10013
212-587-4385

Odyssey House—Adolescent
309–11 E. 6th Street
New York, NY 10003
212-477-9630, Ext. 630

Phoenix House Foundation,
Inc.
164 W. 74th Street
New York, NY 10023
212-595-5810

Daybreak Alcoholism
Treatment Facility
435 E. Henrietta Road
Rochester, NY 14620
716-461-4114

Puerto Rican Youth
Development Center
Proyecto Ayuda Outreach
Program
997 N. Clinton Avenue
Rochester, NY 14621
716-325-3570

136

Lifestart Clinic
1356 Union Street
Schenectady, NY 12308
518-370-0201

Crouse Irving Memorial
  Hospital
Alcohol and Substance
  Abuse Treatment
  Programs
410 S. Crouse Avenue
Syracuse, NY 13210
315-470-7283

Jefferson County Alcohol
  and Substance Abuse
  Council
Globe Mall Court Street
Watertown, NY 13601
315-788-4660

NORTH CAROLINA

Charlotte Council on
  Alcoholism and Chemical
  Dependency, Inc.
100 Billingsley Road
Charlotte, NC 28211
704-376-7447

Durham Drug Counseling
  and Evaluation Services
904 Ramseur Street
Durham, NC 27701
919-688-8244

Sycamore Center
  Prevention/Treatment
101 W. Sycamore Street,
  Suite 410
Greensboro, NC 27401
919-275-9343

Drug Action of Wake
  County, Inc.
Community Treatment
  Project
2809 Industrial Drive
Raleigh, NC 27609
919-832-4453

Cape Fear Substance Center
801 Princess Street
Wilmington, NC 28401
919-343-0145

Step One, Inc.
301 E. 3rd Street
Winston-Salem, NC 27101
919-725-8389

NORTH DAKOTA

West Central Human
  Service Center
Substance Abuse Program
600 S. 2nd Street
Bismarck, ND 58501
701-255-3090

Fargo Clinic Meritcare
  Chemical Dependency
  Program
700 First Avenue South
Fargo, ND 58103
701-234-4000

Dakota Recovery, Inc.
1201 13th Avenue South
Grand Forks, ND 58201
701-722-7203

South Central Human
  Service Center
Alcohol and Drug Abuse
  Program
520 3rd Street
Jamestown, ND 58401
701-252-2641

Northwest Human Service
  Center
Chemical Dependency
  Program
316 2nd Avenue West
Williston, ND 58801
701-572-8126

OHIO

Community Drug Board
725 E. Market Street
Akron, OH 44305
216-434-4141

137

Alcohol and Drug
Assistance, Inc.
1341 Market Avenue North
Canton, OH 44714
216-453-8252

Bethesda Alcohol and Drug
Treatment
619 Oak Street
Cincinnati, OH 45206
513-569-6016

Talbert House
Administrative Office
328 McGregor Street
Cincinnati, OH 45219
513-421-8444

Cleveland Treatment Center,
Inc.
Methadone Clinic
1127 Carnegie Avenue
Cleveland, OH 44115
216-861-4246

Office of Mental Health and
Substance Abuse
Adolescent Counseling
Program
11100 St. Clair Avenue
Cleveland, OH 44108
216-664-2324

Parmadale Chemical
Dependency Services
6753 State Road
Cleveland, OH 44134
216-845-7700

Compdrug Prevention
Program
Youth to Youth
700 Bryden Road
Columbus, OH 43215
614-224-4506

Vita Treatment Center
156 Parsons Avenue, 3rd
Floor
Columbus, OH 43215
614-224-4506

Dayton Free Clinic and
Counseling Center
1133 Salem Avenue
Dayton, OH 45406
513-278-9481

Miami Valley Hospital
Turning Point
Inpatient/Outpatient
1 Wyoming Street
Dayton, OH 45409
513-223-4673

Tri County Addictions
Center Inc.
Outpatient Program
2020 Hayes Avenue
Sandusky, OH 44807
419-625-7262

Substance Abuse Services,
Inc.
2012 Madison Avenue
Toledo, OH 43624
419-243-2168

North Side Medical Center
Adolescent Chemical
Dependency Program
500 Gypsy Lane
Youngstown, OH 44501
216-740-3581

OKLAHOMA

Chemical Dependency
Center
Genesis Outpatient Program
3500 E. Frank Phillips
Boulevard
Bartlesville, OK 74006
918-333-5027

Youth and Family Services
of North Central
Oklahoma, Inc.
2925 N. Midway Street
Enid, OK 73701
405-233-7220

Central Oklahoma CMHC
Substance Abuse Services
909 E. Alameda Street
Norman, OK 73071
405-360-5100

Community Counseling
  Center
2512 S. Harvey St.
Oklahoma City, OK 73109
405-236-3574

Freedom of Choice, Inc.
744 Culbertson Drive
Oklahoma City, OK 73105
405-525-0036

Bright Sky
1508 S. Denver Avenue
Tulsa, OK 74119
918-585-2363

OREGON

Benton/Linn Council on
  Alcohol and Other Drugs
128 S.W. 9th Street
Corvallis, OR 97333
503-758-3000

Chem Free Outpatient
  Services
1247 Villard Street
Eugene, OR 97403
503-342-3767

Lane County
Drug Abuse Treatment
  Program
1901 Garden Avenue
Eugene, OR 97403
503-687-4279

DePaul Center
Youth Treatment Center
4411 N.E. Emerson Street
Portland, OR 97218
503-287-7026

Kaiser Permanente
Adolescent Chemical Health
  Program

2330 N.E. Siskiyou Street
Portland, OR 97212
503-281-4755

White Oaks
3750 Lancaster Drive, N.E.
Salem, OR 97309
503-390-5900

PENNSYLVANIA

Council on Alcohol and
  Drug Abuse
436 N. 6th Street
Allentown, PA 18102
215-437-0801

Holy Spirit Hospital
Substance Abuse Services
N. 21st Street
Camp Hill, PA 17011
717-761-6013

Crozier Chester Medical
  Center
15th Street and Upland
  Avenue
Chester, PA 19013
215-447-2000

Youth Services of Bucks
  County, Inc.
Neshaminy Manor Center
Doylestown, PA 18901
215-343-2800

Hamot Chemical
  Dependency Careunit
201 State Street
Erie, PA 16550
814-870-6133

Addictive Disease Clinic
1727 N. 6th Street
Harrisburg, PA 17102
717-236-9421

Lancaster County Drug and
  Alcohol Program
50 N. Duke Street
Lancaster, PA 17603
717-295-3548

139

Alcohol and Addictions
Council of Delaware
County
12 Veterans Square
Media, PA 19063
215-566-8143

Bridge Adolescent Program
1912 Welsh Road
Philadelphia, PA 19115
215-969-8990

Diagnostic and
Rehabilitation Center
Main Clinic
229 Arch Street
Philadelphia, PA 19106
215-625-8000

Giuffre Medical Center
Girard Avenue and 8th
Street
Philadelphia, PA 19122
215-787-2510

Living Free, Inc.
3514 Kensington Avenue
Philadelphia, PA 19134
215-537-1300

North Central Philadelphia
Commission MH/MR Center
1420 W. Ontario Street
Philadelphia, PA 19140
215-221-8000

Circle C Specialized Group
Home for Chemically
Dependent Adolescents
227 Seabright Street
Pittsburgh, PA 15214
412-323-1727

St. Francis Medical Center
Adolescent Chemical
Dependency Unit
45th and Pennsylvania
Avenue
Pittsburgh, PA 15201
412-622-4601

Berks Youth Counseling
Center
525 Franklin Street
Reading, PA 19602
215-373-4281

Community Medical Center
Substance Abuse Service
1822 Mulberry Street
Scranton, PA 18510
717-969-8781

York Alcohol and Drug
Services, Inc.
211 S. George Street
York, PA 17403
717-854-9591

RHODE ISLAND

Rhode Island Division of
Substance Abuse
Substance Abuse
Detoxification Unit
Rhode Island Medical
Center
Howard Avenue
Cranston, RI 02920
401-464-2531

Community Organization for
Drug Abuse Control
CODAC III
42 Spring Street
Newport, RI 02840
401-846-4150

Pawtucket Alcohol
Counseling Service
104 Broad Street
Pawtucket, RI 02860
401-726-8080

140

Junction Human Service
Corporation
1910 Westminister Street
Providence, RI 02909
401-272-5960

Minority Alcoholism
Program
66 Burnett Street
Providence, RI 02907
401-785-0050

Counseling and Intervention
Services, Inc.
3649 Post Road
Warwick, RI 02889
401-738-1240

SOUTH CAROLINA

Charleston County
Substance Abuse
Commission
25 Courtenay Drive
Charleston, SC 29401
803-723-7212

Lexington/Richland Alcohol
and Drug Abuse Council
2020 Washington Street
Columbia, SC 29204
803-256-3100

Circle Park
Florence County
Commission on Alcohol
and Drug Abuse
P.O. Box 4881
Florence, SC 29502
803-665-9349

Spartanburg County
Commission on Alcohol
and Drug Abuse
131 N. Spring Street
Spartanburg, SC 29301
803-582-7588

Fairfield County
Substance Abuse
Commission

200 Calhoun Street
Winnsboro, SC 29180
803-635-2335

SOUTH DAKOTA

Northern Alcohol/Drug
Referral and Information
Center
22 S.W. 3rd Avenue
Aberdeen, SD 57401
605-225-6131

Brookings Area Alcohol and
Drug Referral Center
509 3rd Avenue
Brookings, SD 57006
605-692-4510

Capital Area Counseling
Service, Inc.
Drug and Alcohol Unit
804 N. Euclid Street
Pierre, SD 57501
605-224-5811

Pennington County
Detoxification Program
924 E. St. Patrick Street
Rapid City, SD 57701
605-394-6128

Carroll Institute
Alcohol and Drug Center
304 S. Phillips Avenue
Sioux Falls, SD 57102
605-336-2556

TENNESSEE

Council on Alcohol and
Drug Abuse Services
207 Spears Avenue
Chattanooga, TN 37405
615-756-7644

Detoxification Rehab
Institute
Adolescent Residential
Treatment
412 Citico Street
Knoxville, TN 37921
615-524-5757

141

Grace House, Inc.
Women's Program
329 N. Bellevue Boulevard
Memphis, TN 38105
901-722-8460

Memphis Adolescent
  Residential Treatment
1170 Vance Avenue
Memphis, TN 38104
901-274-5662

Alcohol and Drug Council
  of Middle Tennessee, Inc.
2612 Westwood Drive
Nashville, TN 37204
615-269-0029

Meharry Community Mental
  Health Center
1005 Dr. D. B. Todd, Jr.,
  Boulevard
Nashville, TN 37208
615-327-1890

TEXAS

Abilene Regional MH/MR
  Center
Human Relations Center
Substance Abuse Services
1174 N. First Street
Abilene, TX 79601
915-673-8106

Panhandle Alcoholic
  Recovery Center
Chemical Abuse Services
Rural Route 3
Amarillo, TX 79107
806-335-2403

Austin Rehabilitation Center
Stratford House
1808 West Avenue
Austin, TX 78701
512-472-8189

Youth Advocacy, Inc.
Youth Advocacy Program
6304-D Porter Street

Austin, TX 78743
512-385-3325

Palmer Drug Abuse Program
Brownsville Inc.
1275 Cottonwood Drive
Brownsville, TX 78520
512-544-3333

Corpus Christi Drug Abuse
  Council
405 Laguna Street
Corpus Christi, TX 78403
512-854-4791

Dallas Challenge
7777 Forest Lane
B-Suite 108
Dallas, TX 75230
214-661-4680

Timberlawn Psychiatric
  Hospital, Inc.
Substance Abuse Services
4600 Samuell Boulevard
Dallas, TX 75227
214-381-7181

Aliviane NO/AD, Inc.
Outpatient Clinic
516A El Paso Drive
El Paso, TX 79905
915-779-3764

Tigua Indian Reservation
Substance Abuse Program
119 S. Old Pueblo Drive
El Paso, TX 79907
915-859-7913

Terrant County Medical
  Education and Research
  Foundation
209 W. Magnolia Avenue
Fort Worth, TX 76104
817-921-2262

St. Mary's Hospital
Substance Abuse Program
404 St. Mary's Boulevard
Galveston, TX 77550
409-763-5301, Ext. 4302

142

Association for the
Advancement of Mexican
Americans
Alcohol/Drug Program
204 Clifton Street
Houston, TX 77011
713-926-9491, Ext. 13

Gulf Coast Community
Services Association
Substance Abuse Services
Program
6300 Bowling Green Street,
Suite 143
Houston, TX 77021
713-748-4410, Ext. 773

Westbranch Treatment
Center
2005 Jacquelyn Street
Houston, TX 77055
713-682-2566

Lubbock Regional MH/MR
Center
1210 Texas Avenue
Lubbock, TX 79401
806-766-0237

Permian Basin Center for
Battered Women and their
Children
Midland, TX 79702
915-683-1300

Bexar County MH/MR
Center
Crisis Stabilization Unit
1214 W. Poplar Street
San Antonio, TX 78207
512-225-5481

Mexican American Unity
Council, Inc.
Casa Del Sol/Casa Adelante
Residential Treatment
Program
2303 W. Commerce Street,
Suite 300
San Antonio, TX 78207
512-225-4117

San Antonio Youth Services
Division
Substance Abuse Prevention
Program
115 Plaza de Armas Street,
Suite 151C
San Antonio, TX 78285
512-299-7191

Heart of Texas MH/MR
Substance Abuse Program
110 S. 12th Street
Waco, TX 76703
817-752-3451, Ext. 308

UTAH

Logan Regional Hospital
Dayspring
1400 N. 500 East
Logan, UT 84321
801-752-2050, Ext. 5275

Weber Department of
Alcohol and Drug Abuse
2650 Lincoln Avenue
Ogden, UT 84401
801-625-3650

Utah Alcoholism
Foundation
Central Division
1726 South Dakota Lane
Provo, UT 84601
801-373-6562

Odyssey House, Inc.
Juvenile Treatment Program
625 S. 200 East
Salt Lake City, UT 84111
801-363-0203

Salt Lake County
Alcoholism and Drug Abuse
Services Division
2001 S. State Street, Suite
2300
Salt Lake City, UT 84190
801-468-2009

143

Uintah Basin Counseling,
Inc.
559 N. 1700 West
Vernal, UT 84078
801-781-0743

VERMONT

Marathon House
101 Western Avenue
Brattleboro, VT 05301
802-257-1147

Champlain Drug and
Alcohol Services
45 Clarke Street
Burlington, VT 05401
802-862-5243

Howard Mental Health
Services
Substance Abuse Unit
300 Flynn Avenue
Burlington, VT 05401
802-658-0404

Washington County
Youth Services Bureau, Inc.
38 Elm Street
Montpelier, VT 05602
802-229-9151

Vermont Office of Alcohol
and Drug Abuse Programs
District Office
165 Lake Street
St. Albans, VT 05478
802-527-1717

VIRGINIA

Outpatient Counseling
Program
517 N. St. Asaph Street
Alexandria Health
Department
Alexandria, VA 22314
703-838-5066

Arlington Alcohol and Drug
Program
South 16th Street Center
3025 S. 16th Street
Arlington, VA 22204
703-920-3410

Alternatives
12284 Warwick Boulevard,
Suite 2D
Newport News, VA 23606
804-596-7670

Norfolk Drug Treatment
Services
2811-C Lafayette Boulevard
Norfolk, VA 23509
804-857-1155

The Harbours
Chemical Dependency
Recovery Program
301 Fort Lane
Portsmouth, VA 23704
804-634-0440, Ext. 610

Richmond Aftercare, Inc.
Men's and Women's
Programs
1109 Bainbridge Street
Richmond, VA 23224
804-231-5592

Rubicon, Inc.
1300 Mactavish Avenue
Richmond, VA 23230
804-359-3255

MH Services of Roanoke
Valley
New Directions
Treatment/Prevention/Intervention
1345 Clarke Avenue, S.W.
Roanoke, VA 24016
703-343-2425

Comprehensive Substance
Abuse Program
Pembroke Six, Suite 126
Virginia Beach, VA 23462
804-499-5401

WASHINGTON

Youth Eastside Services
16150 8th Street, N.E.
Bellevue, WA 98008
206-747-4937

Kitsap County Council on
    Alcoholism
532 5th Street
Bremerton, WA 98310
206-377-0051

Evergreen Manor, Inc.
Evergreen
    Alcohol/Substance Abuse
    Outpatient Program
2617 Summit Avenue
Everett, WA 98201
206-258-2407

St. Peter Hospital
Chemical Dependency
    Program
413 N. Lilly Road
Olympia, WA 98506
206-456-7575

Center for Human Services
Juvenile Drug Abuse
    Program
17011 Meridian Avenue
    North
Seattle, WA 98133
206-546-2411

Therapeutic Health
    Services, Inc.
1116 Summit Avenue
Seattle, WA 98101
206-323-0930

Spokane CMHC Drug
    Program
Center for Drug Treatment
1625 West 4th Avenue
Spokane, WA 99204
509-458-7437

Stepps Clinic
Outpatient Drug Counseling
    Service

1101 College Avenue West,
    Suite 360
Spokane, WA 99201
509-326-9550

Olympic Counseling
    Services
223 N. Yakima Street
Lutheran Services Building
Tacoma, WA 98403
206-272-3454

Central Washington
    Comprehensive Mental
    Health Drug Program
321 E. Yakima Avenue
Yakima, WA 98901
509-575-4084

WEST VIRGINIA

Charleston Area Medical
    Center
Adolescent and Adult Care
    Units
Brooks and Washington
    Streets
Charleston, WV 25301
304-348-6066

Shawnee Hills Community
    MH/MR Center, Inc.
Substance Abuse Services
511 Morris Street
Charleston, WV 25301
304-345-4800

Appalachian Mental Health
    Center
Alcoholism and Drug Abuse
    Program
Wilmouth and Yokum
    Streets
Elkins, WV 26241
304-636-3232

Western District Guidance
    Center, Inc.
Substance Abuse Program
2121 7th Street
Parkersburg, WV 26101
304-485-1721

Northern Panhandle
  Behavioral Health Center
New Hope Program
2121 Eoff Street
Wheeling, WV 26003
304-233-6250

WISCONSIN

Community Alcoholism
  Services
217 S. Badger Avenue
Appleton, WI 54914
414-731-6414

L. E. Phillips Treatment
  Center for the Chemically
  Dependent
2661 County Trunk I
Chippewa Falls, WI 54729
715-723-5585

Brown County Mental
  Health Center
Alcoholism and Drug Abuse
  Services
2900 St. Anthony Drive
Green Bay, WI 54301
414-468-1136, Ext. 422

William Olcott and
  Associates
Outpatient Substance
  Services
415 S. Washington Street
Green Bay, WI 54305
414-433-9414

Kenosha Youth
  Development Services
Substance Abuse Program
5407 8th Avenue
Kenosha, WI 53140
414-656-6788

St. Francis Community
  Programs, Inc.
922 Ferry Street
La Crosse, WI 54601
608-637-7055

Apogee
300 Femrite Drive
Madison, WI 53716
608-222-7311

New Start Program of
  Meriter Hospital
Outpatient Clinic
1605 Monroe Street
Madison, WI 53711
608-258-8700

De Paul Central Clinic
2601 N. Martin Luther King
  Drive
Milwaukee, WI 53212
414-265-3388

Milwaukee Council on Drug
  Abuse
1442 N. Farwell Avenue
Milwaukee, WI 53202
414-271-7822

WYOMING

The Prairie Institute, Inc.
1236 S. Elm Street
Casper, WY 82601
307-266-2580

Cheyenne Community Drug
  Abuse Treatment Council,
  Inc.
Pathfinder
803 W. 21st Street
Cheyenne, WY 82001
307-635-0256

Southwest Wyoming
  Alcoholism Rehabilitation
  Association
430 S. Jackson Street
Jackson, WY 83001
307-733-5332

Southeast Wyoming Mental
  Health Center
Albany County Branch
710 Garfield, No. 320
Laramie, WY 82070
307-734-8915

Northern Wyoming Mental
   Health Center Substance
   Abuse Services
1221 W. 5th Street
Sheridan, WY 82801
307-674-4405

SOURCE NOTES

Chapter One: America's War on Drugs

1. According to a survey by the National Institute on Drug Abuse, there was a 37 percent decline in the number of Americans using illegal drugs on a "current" basis (at least once in the previous month) during the years 1985–88. That means the estimated 23 million casual users in 1985 had been reduced to about 14 million in 1988. However, the same study revealed that the number of people becoming addicted to cocaine and crack, the smokable form of cocaine, rose dramatically. While 647,000 survey respondents reported using cocaine once a week in 1985, the number jumped to 862,000 by 1988. The number of daily cocaine users rose by nearly 50,000 in that same time period.

2. The Washington, D.C.–based Crime Control Institute reported that in 1988, fourteen police officers were killed in incidents involving drugs. This was the highest number on record since 1972, the year statistics were first collected. The fourteen slayings, all by gunshot, comprised nearly one-fifth of all police deaths in 1988.

3. *HIV Infection and Disease*, edited by Norbert Rapoza. The American Medical Association, 1989.

4. Ibid.

Chapter Two: Treatment Options for Drug Dependency

1. Narcotics Anonymous is a registered trademark of World Service Office, Inc.

Chapter Four: Methadone Maintenance Treatment

1. Within the methadone maintenance community, the goal of drug-free living is seen as realistic for some addicts and unrealistic for others. The differences between these two approaches have important implications for the way a methadone program is administered.

Methadone patients seeking eventual drug-free living typically receive lower doses of methadone, undergo withdrawal counseling, and work toward more thorough resocialization. In long-term methadone maintenance programs, patients are encouraged to develop job talents and other skills that will enable them to stabilize their lives. Since there is no goal of abstinence, these patients are given higher methadone dosages to deter their continued use of heroin and they do not undergo a withdrawal program. Federal regulations allow both treatment approaches.

2. James R. Cooper, "Methadone treatment and acquired immunodeficiency syndrome," *Journal of the American Medical Association*, September 22/29, 1989 (Vol. 262, No. 12, Pages 1664–1668).

FOR FURTHER READING

Berger, Gilda. *Drug Abuse: The Impact on Society.* New York: Franklin Watts, 1988.

Cohen, Daniel and Cohen, Susan. *A Six-Pack and a Fake I.D.: Teens Look at the Drinking Question.* New York: M. Evans, 1988.

Drug, Alcohol, and Other Addictions: A Directory of Treatment Centers and Prevention Programs Nation- wide. Phoenix, AZ: Oryx Press, 1989.

Hubbard, Robert L.; Marsden, Mary Ellen; Rachal, J. Valley; Harwood, Henrick J.; Cavanaugh, Elizabeth R; Ginzburg, Harold M. *Drug Abuse Treatment: A National Study of Effectiveness.* Chapel Hill, NC: The University of North Carolina Press, 1989.

Inaba, Darryl S. and Cohen, William E. *Uppers, Downers and All Arounders.* Ashland, OR: Cinemed, 1989.

U.S. Department of Health and Human Services Public Health Service. (DHHS Publication No. [ADM] 89–1603.) *National Directory of Drug Abuse and Alcoholism Treatment and Prevention Programs.* Washington, DC: U.S. Government Printing Office, 1989.

INDEX

Bush, George H., 15–17

Camareno, Ricardo, 25
Center for Disease Control, 26, 27, 28
Chamberland, Mary E., 28
Citizens Crime Commission (N.Y.C.), 24
Coca, 34
Coca-Cola, 35
Cocaine, 34, 35, 95. *See also* Crack cocaine
Cocaine addiction, 93–96: extent of, 91; among high school students, 92; physical effects of, 93–94
Cocaine Anonymous, 36, 99
Cocaine epidemic, 91–100
Codependency, 53
Colombian drug cartels, 29
Controlled environment, 98
Cooper, James R., 71
Crack cocaine, 20, 91–92; and available treatment, 96; fast addiction of, 93; and high school students, 92. *See also* Cocaine
Crime Control Institute, 24, 149n2

Department of Health and Human Services (U.S.), 21
Department of Human Services (IA), 75
Detoxification, 50
Detroit, 23
Diagnostic and Rehab Center (Philadelphia), 93
Dissociative anesthetics, 20
Diversion, 69
Dole, Vincent, 61
Dopamine, 94
Dope Cola, 35
Downers, 20
Drug abuse and abusers: cost of, 42–43; deaths caused by, 23–24; by gender, 22; getting a handle on, 19–23; variety of, 41
Drug addiction, 35–36; moral explanations of, 65; and physical imbalance, 64–65
Drug Czar, 11
Drug dependency, 33–46
Drug Enforcement Agency (U.S.), 70
Drug replacement theory, 62, 64
Drugs and drug use: attempted cures for, 34–36; casual use of,

N.A., 107–111; and spiritual principles, 107; and Woodlands program, 83, 86

Univ. of Iowa, 13
Uppers, 20

Warden, Julie, 76, 77, 82, 85
War on Drugs: crime connection of, 23–25; founding (1989), 11; and mobilization of United States, 31; motivating, 23–31; and risk to society, 28–31; and treatment/ prevention programs, 59
Washington, D.C., 23
Woodlands Treatment Program, 75–76, 83– 90; action phase of, 88; Christian foundations of, 85; costs of, 84–85; and education, 80–81; exploration phase of, 87–88; family days, 89; and focus on specifics, 79–80; Forces Paper of, 86–87; and habilitation, 81–82; intake phase of, 86; levels of treatment in, 84; patient profile, 90; real world phase of, 89–90; transition phase of, 88–89
World Health Organization, 27

Young House Family Services Inc., 76

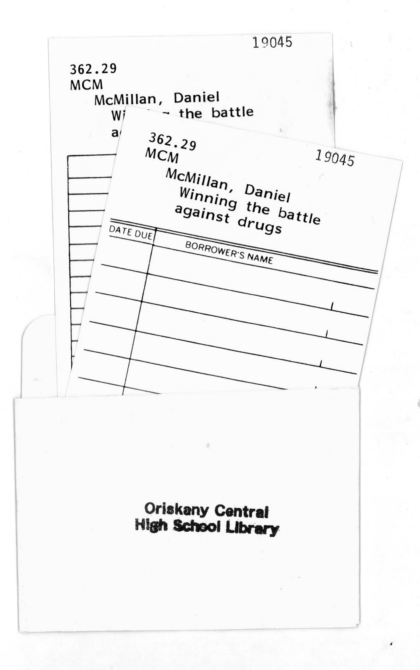